As they sat side by side on
the wagon seat, with the
hastily built box holding the
body of their child, Papa said,
"She won't be alone, Mama;
there have been so many
graves before hers this winter."
"I wonder if the doctors will
ever find a cure for diphtheria?"
Mama's voice was doubtful,
and she thought of the five
other small ones at home.
Once again she felt the stir of
the new life near her heart.
Funny how each child became
someone special, filling a need
in the family's lives.

The Preacher Had 10 Kids

FRANCES BRADSHER

LIVING BOOKS
Tyndale House Publishers, Inc.
Wheaton, Illinois

Acknowledgments and Dedication
My gratitude goes to so many who
have helped with this book: The
Park City Daily News of Bowling
Green, Kentucky, which furnished
me with data and photographs; Pat
Hodges, Manuscript Division, Ken-
tucky Library, Western Kentucky
University, Bowling Green, Ken-
tucky, who helped me with excerpts
from both the library and The
Southern Educator; Journal of the
Louisville Conference, furnished by
L. W. Woodward; and for the part
in "Nannie" excerpted from "I
Remember Nannie" with special
permission of Farm Journal, Inc.,
copyright 1954.

My thanks too, for the stories
shared by Papa's relatives and his
friends..

Most of all this book is dedicated
to all the grandchildren, especially
to Cherry and Betsy who lived for
awhile under Papa's own vine and
fig tree and who will always hold in
their hearts a loving memory of
those times.

Second printing, October 1981

Library of Congress
Catalog Card Number 79-93234
ISBN 0-8423-4886-7, paper

CONTENTS

The Cherry Tree

GEORGE WASHINGTON CHERRY "Mr. George" 1822-1911
MARTHA FRANCES STAHL "Marthy" 1852-1919

Nine sons:

Jeremiah Taylor Cherry, "Jerry" 1852-1936 Minister
Isaac, "Ike" 1854-1918 Farmer
John W., 1856-1912 Teacher
Allen, 1857-1881 Farmer
William Bailey, "Bale" 1860-1921 Farmer
Thomas Crittenden, "T.C." 1862-1947 Teacher
Henry Hardin, "H.H." 1864-1937
Teacher, founder of Western Kentucky University,
Bowling Green, Ky.
George W., 1867-1936 Lawyer
Redford Columbus, 1871-1917 Lawyer

JEREMIAH TAYLOR CHERRY "Jerry" 1852-1936
LEONA CELESTE WHITE "Lestle" 1857-1944

Ten Children:

Ira Ithiel Thaddeus 1877- (date of death unknown)
Ariel Clarence 1878-1961
Zephaniah Taylor "Zeph" 1880- (date of death unknown)
Ulalia Roxanna "Roxy" 1882-1888
Mary Martha "Sister" 1885-1929
David Ella "Spooks" 1887-1976
Nellie Grace "Nell" 1889-1922
Elizabeth Elliott "Ibbie" 1890-
Katherine Celeste 1893-1911
Frances Willard 1899-

Introduction

THIS is the story of Kentucky as I remember it from the time of my birth in 1899 until I was twenty-one in 1920. It is the story of my father Jeremiah Taylor Cherry, a Methodist minister in the Louisville Conference, whose mother, Martha Stahl Cherry, knew before he was born what his calling would be.

The tale includes Leona Celeste White, my mother, and her ten children, born from December 1876 to July 25, 1899. Papa gave us these names: Ithiel Thaddeus, Ariel Clarence, Zephaniah Taylor, Ulalia Roxanna, Mary Martha, David Ella, Nellie Grace, Elizabeth Elliott, and Katherine Celeste. I was the redheaded last child, number ten, and my title, Frances Willard, honored the famous female temperance pioneer of that day.

My earliest recollections are of moving almost yearly to a new Kentucky town: Franklin, Trenton, Elkton, Russellville, Calhoun, Jeffersontown, Sebree, and back to Elkton. We were dressed out of the "missionary barrel." I can still smell those musty, outdated clothes; I hated them.

We ate well when our parishioners' crops were good, but we lived on their meager surplus when times were bad; one drought year our "quarterage" consisted almost entirely of turnips, and it took me from then until my present age of eighty to be able to stomach a turnip again!

Life in Kentucky today is far different from my Kentucky of the early 1900s. I have tried to recapture the essence of the times and the people as well as I can.

1

Roots

IT was that eerie time just before dawn that hids a lingering goodbye to night as if reluctant to beckon in another day. Tentative shafts of light from the rising sun began to appear through the trees beside the rutted road. A farewell blast from the packet, the *Bowling Green*, came from upriver. Papa and I were the only passengers she had unloaded at Mouth of Gasper, the nearest stop to Grandfather George Washington Cherry's house.

I was ten at the time, the youngest of ten children. This was my first trip by water, for Papa had pastored inland churches in Kentucky since I could remember.

An hour earlier Papa had awakened me in full dark and helped me down from the upper bunk bed where I had been sleeping.

"Time to get off the boat," he told me.

I fumbled into my clothes and followed Papa to the upper deck. Below us we could see the roustabouts lowering the gangplank to the bank. The *Bowling*

Green was making a mighty backward churning of paddle wheels to keep the packet from coming too close to shore. One of the deck hands held a lighted lantern to see us safely to solid ground.

Once there, we seemed to be entering some unknown land of semidarkness and rustling leaves. The banks of the Barren River were less steep now, leveling off into gentle slopes.

The day before as we had left Green River to enter the Barren, the steep, rocky cliffs had loomed up. Sometimes to my ten-year-old eyes, the crags seemed to enclose us from three sides. There were caves in the shaly bluffs and I imagined living there alone, fishing the river and eating wild berries and nuts, sharing my home with some friendly animal. My large family left me with little time by myself, and the prospect of a solitary life had intrigued me for the moment.

But right now I was glad to hold Papa's hand and he, sensing my uneasiness, started to show me things with which he had been familiar as a boy. He pointed to a big tree outlined against the rising sun.

"That old tree has furnished us with bushels of scaly-bark hickory nuts," he told me. "I expect Aunt Jane is saving some for you." My mouth watered at the thought of scaly-barks, with a shell so thin the smallest rock could open it and release the fat goodies inside!

We started up the road, walking single file in the ruts, for underbrush had almost filled the center. Papa looked so tall and protective as he led the way. I tried to stay close behind, and I noticed that Papa's usual long strides had been shortened so that I had little trouble keeping up.

"Farmers used to bring their produce down this

road to the boat landing," Papa told me. "I've driven many a yoke of oxen with a wagonload of potatoes or corn. Sometimes I'd have a load of wood for the boats to burn."

We had seen the *Bowling Green* being loaded and unloaded at the stops between Calhoun and the Mouth of Gasper. At most places the produce, unless it was livestock, had been left on the bank unattended until it was picked up by the boat.

Day was lighting the world now, and I was getting tired.

"How far is it to Grandma's?" I asked. "I'm getting thirsty."

We were on a rise in the road and Papa turned off into a narrow path leading down into a hollow. It was shaded by trees and brush. The caw of an early-rising crow split the air. Papa stopped.

"Listen."

I could hear the sound of running water and saw below our path a hollow log embedded in the rock wall. A stream of water flowed out of the other end of the log. Papa reached into a bush and took down a long handled gourd dipper. He rinsed it several times, filled it, and handed the water to me.

It was as cold as ice, and I drank thirstily. Papa drank too. "Couldn't count the times I've had a drink from that spring. Tasted pretty good after a hard day's work in a hot field."

Ferns grew beside the little stream that flowed from the log. Some small creature scurried through the brush. Birds were tuning up for their morning songs as they flew from tree to tree. I stood still for a moment, awed by the majesty of the woodland, which seemed to stretch endlessly about me on all sides. I wondered how many people from long ago, tired and thirsty, had passed by this spot and been refreshed.

Papa led me up the path to the top of the hill, past Grandfather Cherry's big barn, which stood behind the house. The minty scent of pennyroyal was strong here, the plant which furnished that section of Kentucky with its nickname, "Pennyrile."

We walked past the barn and approached the house of hand-hewn logs which Grandfather had built with the help of Papa and his brothers after they had gotten big enough for such work. Until that time, they had lived in the smaller cabin which had stood near the present site. After the larger house had been built, the old one was torn down.

There were four huge rooms in the front, two upstairs, two down, with a wide hall between. There were two doors in the hall, one opened onto the front porch, the other onto the back stoop, which ran across the back of my grandparents' room on the left, and down beside the ell-shaped rooms. The ell consisted of a closed dogtrot and a large kitchen which could be entered from the bedroom. In the summer the dogtrot was used as a dining room, with a long plank table which could seat twenty people on its benches. There were two chimneys, one at the end of each of the two front rooms. They were built from sandstone rocks from the farm, and held together with homemade mortar that often had to be rechinked.

The kitchen had a flue for Grandma's wood-burning step stove, and there were few times when a wisp of smoke could not be seen coming out of it.

A stoop, or narrow porch outside the left front room and ell had steps leading into the backyard. It made a dry place to hang strings of hot peppers and herbs.

The path to the log smokehouse behind the kitchen was paved with flat stones. You only had to count three steps before you could smell the smoky goodness of the old hams and sacked sausage hanging there.

You entered the front rooms from the hall, either from the front porch or the back stoop. A wide stairway in the downstairs hall led to the hall above and adjoining bedroom. The wall of the other bedroom was solid with no access from the hall. This special room was always reserved for girls, and could only be entered through the parents' bedroom. (Since there were no girls in the Cherry family, Aunt Jane had this one.)

This room was reached by a narrow stairway in the corner. There were two steps up, a small platform, then steep ladderlike steps leading up at right angles. Under the stairway was a closet which held special treats such as lard for cakes and cookies, preserves made with loaf sugar instead of honey and syrup, and late apples saved at the last minute from a freeze.

As we neared the house, chickens were scratching in the back yard, but at Papa's "Hello!" they fled squawking under the porch. At the sound of Papa's greeting, Grandfather Cherry came from the kitchen and stood on the stoop. His six-foot-two-inch height never failed to awe me; he was even taller than Papa, and his piercing dark eyes could look through a child and see all the hidden evil she was trying to conceal. His hair and full beard were white. He always walked with a gnarled cane, for which I had a deep respect— with reason. It was his corrective weapon.

Grandmother Cherry, so tiny she barely reached his shoulder, came out and stood beside him. Her hair was pulled back from her small face in a severe knot and, on seeing us, her blue eyes filled with tears. When Papa took her into his arms the tears ran down her face, and she wiped them off with the hem of her checked gingham apron. I never saw Grandma cry except when she was happy. Grandfather offered his hand to Papa, then to me. "Well, Jerry, I'm glad you finally got here. It will probably be the last time you will ever see me alive; I've been so poorly." This, I learned, was his standard greeting for his remaining years, when he died at the ripe old age of eighty-nine.

A hug from Grandma and her usual, "How you're growing, Willard," made me feel at home. We went into the kitchen where Aunt Jane (really no kin to us at all) was standing at the stove. She held out her hand to Papa, but he took her into his arms and gave her a hug.

"Aw, Jerry," she lisped, turning to offer me her soft cheek for a kiss.

I had been rude the first time I saw Aunt Jane, some years before this visit. Her upper lip was entirely gone, and a marble of flesh grew from the end of her nose. Four missing upper teeth made her chewing clearly visible. I lost my appetite and hurriedly left the table.

Later I wandered outside and sat under the shade of a tree. My stomach was demanding food. I heard a step behind me and saw a hand reaching over my shoulder. It held two biscuits, one centered with a piece of old ham, the other dappled with butter and blackberry jam.

"Reckoned you'd be hongry by now." It was Aunt

Jane, and never again did I see her except through eyes of love.

Aunt Jane went to the stove, opened the oven, and there lay brown biscuits which seemed to be trying their best to turn upside down from their very lightness. A skillet of old ham sizzled and in a pan at the back I saw guinea eggs simmering. Aunt Jane remembered how I liked them peeled while hot and covered with redeye gravy.

After a hurried hand-wash outside on the stoop and a quick drying on the rough roller towel, we sat down at the long kitchen table. I was hungry, and hoped Papa wouldn't go into one of his impressive sermon-blessings while the biscuits cooled. He must have been hungry too, for he only said,

"We thank thee, our heavenly Father, for these and all thy blessings. For Christ's sake, Amen."

Aunt Jane began to fill our plates. It was hard to decide, after the ham, eggs, and biscuits, which jelly or preserves to choose from. Maybe the honey from Grandfather's beehives or the thick sorghum from his sugar cane? Unable to decide, I started out by cutting lavishly into the big round of fresh churned butter which was near my plate.

2

Aunt Jane

VISITS to Grandmother's house were frequent. My Grandfather George Cherry, Grandma "Marthy," and Aunt Jane sat around the big fireplace in the winter. Grandmother was usually knitting socks to rest her eyes, Aunt Jane mending or shelling dried beans or peas, Grandfather rocking slowly, gazing into the fire.

Grandfather believed to the day he died that a man was head of his household, and implicit obedience was expected from everyone who entered his home. He followed the "spare the rod" rule and his heavy, knotted walking stick was his scepter of power. I never saw him without it. Although he stood as straight as when he was young, he depended, I secretly thought, on the stick's moral support.

Each evening just before bedtime Grandma reached up on the high mantel and took down her corncob pipe, which she filled with home-grown tobacco and lit with a coal from the hearth. "Helps my asthmy," she explained, puffing away contentedly.

We got up in the morning and went to bed at night at Grandfather's signal, even if there happened to be one more thread to pull through a stocking being darned or one last puff left in Grandma's pipe.

It was by the fireplace that I heard stories of my

ancestors on both sides, of the marriage of Grandfather and "Marthy," the birth of the nine Cherry sons, and their early years.

Little was ever said about where Aunt Jane lived before she came to stay in the Cherry household, except that she had come when quite young to help "Mr. George" and "Marthy" with the endless work on the farm. It wasn't unusual in those days to take in an orphan girl for her board and keep, but Grandmother's goodness in looking after the harelipped servant was the subject of much discussion and praise. At that time scant care was provided for any orphan. One as disfigured as Jane would have lived a hopeless life with any relative who would tolerate her, knowing that no man would ever consider her as a wife, which was every girl's ambition. Other careers were almost unheard of.

The first day at Grandfather Cherry's, Aunt Jane set the table with two plates, expecting as she always had to wait for whatever scraps that might be left.

Grandma had added another plate and said, "Jane, you are part of the family now." And part of the family she was. These people were her people. She had her own warm bed, instead of a pallet, in her own room over my grandparents' room.

Grandmother was noted for her even disposition, but she confessed to me (out of Grandfather's hearing) that much of it was due to Aunt Jane's habit of "shunting" work off her shoulders. It was Aunt Jane who rose at the crack of dawn and went to the kitchen to make the fire. She saved Grandmother countless steps and furnished her with many a stolen early morning nap while Grandfather unsuspectingly went about the outside chores. Grandmother treated

Aunt Jane like a loved sister. Every year she was allowed to have her own brood of chickens, and her own garden was set aside.

As the years went by, Aunt Jane became second mother to the boys. It was she who took each small child into her own bed when his place between his mother and father had been usurped by a new baby. It was she who comforted the child in her straight chair before the fireplace while Marthy rocked the new little one.

All the boys and the grandchildren remembered the cookies she made and kept in a crock in the staircase closet. How she made them to keep fresh so long remains a mystery. Some special sweet cakes had a raisin in the center. These were reserved for the child who had received an especially hard whaling at Grandfather's hands. It must have hurt Grandmother, who punished the boys by holding their heads between her small knees while they were in a kneeling position and applying her small hands to their upturned backsides. Papa often told how the boys laughed silently during the process, then wiped their eyes to feign tears.

It was Aunt Jane who saw to it that Grandfather always had the fried dried apple or peach pie he demanded for his breakfast every morning. During long afternoons in the summer, she and Grandma sat outside under the trees peeling the fruit and cutting it into small pieces to be dried in the sun on top of the smokehouse, later to be hung in sacks under the rafters.

It was Aunt Jane who carefully smoked the hog meat, gathering hickory chips from the woodpile to add to the proper bits of apple wood which gave the cured meat its special flavor. Each head of a household had his own special formula for smoking meat. I remember so well the tender three-year-old hams they saved to be served at family reunions and to guests.

It would be hard to estimate the gallons of jellies and preserves Aunt Jane and Grandmother made each summer. Most of it was stored in stone crocks, each topped with a clean cloth and plate and kept in a cool place in the cellar. The homemade sorghum was kept in a barrel in the smokehouse, and it was fun to go with Aunt Jane and see it flow from the spout in the side. The flow was fast in hot weather, but it froze solid in winter and had to be cut in blocks. A chunk put inside a hot buttered biscuit and allowed to partially melt made superb eating.

The beehives were kept in the orchard and supplied the family with sweetening both for the table and for preserves, which were served in glass compotes Grandma's mother had brought over from Germany. They sparkled with lights as the sun touched the dish.

Aunt Jane did the churning too, and worked the butter into the big round cakes that a small person felt free to cut into lavishly, breaking our usual habit at home of slivering off a minute slice.

Late every evening, Aunt Jane would come in the back door with her apron held in one hand to make a sack. The sack was full of eggs, many of them found in out-of-the-way fence corners or in the roots of a tree. The hens had a way of trying to hide a batch of eggs so they could raise a brood of chicks. They took pride in bringing their surprise family into the yard, and woe to the animal or child who disturbed them! New mother hens fought with sharp wing feathers, beaks, and claws to protect their young.

Sometimes Aunt Jane's apron would hold fresh fruit from the orchard or chips from the woodpile for starting the fires. (Grandmother always lit a chip fire in the fireplace, even in the hottest summer weather! She said, "It is healthy to take out the dampness.") Jane's aprons were sometimes stained from wild grapes she had found unexpectedly in the woods.

At hog-killing time she stood over the big iron kettle stirring the bits of fat to see that each batch of lard was just right for whatever use it was intended. The solid, or leaf fat was reserved for making her cakes and cookies, and she kept it hidden in the stairway closet for that purpose.

On Sunday meeting days she stayed home, though the family urged her to attend the service with them. When everyone got back, always with other members or visitors from the church, they found a bountiful spread waiting them, with Aunt Jane in the kitchen keeping the food hot for each new onslaught of appetites.

Tending to the chickens was her special task. She saw to it that broody hens found a safe nest for their eggs, and when the little chicks were hatched, she stood over them at feeding time to see that they were not overrun and robbed of their crumbs of cornbread.

If Aunt Jane had any formal religion no one ever heard her confess it. Nell and Elizabeth, two of my older sisters, tell of the time before Katherine was born when they had been sent to Grandma's. Babies were born at home, and children were not supposed to know where they came from, so a trip at this time was the custom.

Both girls became desperately homesick, and on a trip to the barn Aunt Jane heard them praying, "God, if you really are God, let us go home." The little girls were crying. Aunt Jane slipped out and in a few days Papa got a letter. (How she ever learned to write we never knew.)

Dere Jerry:

If you want yore girls to believe in God you'd better come and get them. Jane.

Papa came and got them the day he got the letter.

As each Cherry boy left home to make his way in the world, Aunt Jane gave him two gifts. One was a white shirt, the other two linen handkerchiefs, carefully made from store-bought material. Papa said the gifts gave them courage to face the outside world.

From someone came the rumor that when my Uncle Redford Columbus was a teenager he had planned to run away from home. Grandfather had administered an extra form of discipline for some disobedience, and the boy was smarting both inside and out. The family knew his anger, but it was Aunt Jane who took him to the fireplace, uncovered a crock of buckwheat batter to make pancakes for breakfast next morning (they were Redford's favorite food), and let him smell the special hickory bark syrup warming to one side.

Redford stayed at home until the time came to leave with Grandfather's blessing and with the earnings from his last year on the farm. He became district attorney in Bardstown and a well-known and respected lawyer.

The other eight boys were fed buckwheat cakes and raisin cookies by Aunt Jane in times of stress, and it must have worked. Papa went into the ministry; Isaac

L. became a prosperous farmer; George W., a prominent attorney in Washington and California; John W., a teacher; Allen, who died in his twenties, a farmer; William Bailey stayed on the farm and became the local arbitrator in disputes; Thomas Crittenden became superintendent of Warren County schools and in 1935 wrote *Kentucky—The Pioneer State of the West*, a history textbook. Henry Hardin, who, as he entered Bowling Green driving an oxcart of potatoes, saw the vision of a normal school for teachers on the hill outside town, lived to see his dream realized. His statue, cast in bronze, now stands on the campus (now Western Kentucky University).

Early Years

IT was a privilege to sit before Grandfather Cherry's big fireplace and listen to the family as they reminisced about events in the past. Grandfather George was an avid reader, a good storyteller, and he expressed his views on many subjects. The rumor was being spread that some kind of horseless vehicle was being invented. (Grandfather George's snort at this absurdity made me a disbeliever, too, until I saw my first automobile some years later.) "Ha!" Grandfather would exclaim, looking around for our nods of approval. "Imagine a buggy running down the road without a horse or mule to pull it! Absurd!"

We heard, too, about our ancestors, for Grandfather was proud of his heritage. The first Cherrys came to this continent from Antrim County, Ireland. They claimed to be descendants of the Duke of Wellington. Zachary Taylor, Grandfather George said, was from the branch of the Taylors that was related to both the Cherrys and the Whites, Mama's people.

Grandfather George's great-grandfather, William Cherry, had fought in the Revolutionary War. Later his own grandfather had moved to North Carolina where Grandfather Cherry's father William was born. Grandfather Cherry grew up in North Carolina, moved to Kentucky when he was grown, and settled near Barren River.

With such a background, Grandfather looked around for a suitable wife when time came to marry. Martha Frances Stahl, of good German stock on her father's side, and Scotch Irish on the Taylor side (as nearly as I could find out, Grandmother and Grandfather were second cousins), was his choice. There were not too many girls in the vicinity who were in his class.

A daguerrotype of Grandma when she was young explained in part Grandfather Cherry's choice, though he would have snorted at the idea that her petite size and good looks had anything to do with his decision.

Grandmother Marthy was sixteen when they married on April 29, 1850, and he brought her to the cabin where their nine boys were born.

From the start, the farm was almost self-supporting. Bees were brought from his father's farm in North Carolina, and a start of livestock was also given to him. He planted fruit trees, and the orchard on the place grew to several acres. There was always fruit in abundance there. Sometimes it was hard to decide which kind of fruit to choose.

After I was old enough to hear about babies my grandmother—Martha Stahl Cherry—told me about the cold winter day when Papa was born. The cabin had been clay chinked against the threat of such weather when this event occurred, but the icy wind still found its way into the room. She told about watching "Mr. George," her name for my grandfather, as he laid big logs on the fire. He kept an anxious eye on her as she lay, almost lost in the big feather bed.

Aunt Jane bathed her face, wet from sweat, for the labor had been a long and hard one.

"What time is it?" Martha asked.

Mr. George pulled his big watch out of his pocket and looked at it by firelight. "Almost midnight," he told her.

"If he waits a little longer he will be a February 29th baby." Grandma said she prayed for this in spite of the pain. She knew her first son was a special called-of-God child—that he would be a Methodist minister. He deserved a set-apart birthday.

Papa waited for the twenty-ninth before his lusty cry filled the room. Aunt Jane wrapped him in a homespun blanket and laid him in Grandma's arms. She looked into his face, feeling one with Hannah, who had so long ago dedicated her son Samuel to the Lord.

Next day the baby was named. During the months of Grandma's pregnancy Grandfather had spent a lot of time going over family names as well as names in the Bible, looking for a proper one for his son. Never once did he add a girl's name to his list. When Grandma heard some of the names she had to hide a smile.

As Grandfather approached the bed with the list in his hand, Grandmother waited for him to call them off. She had never learned to read, but she could pick up the Bible and read any passage she wanted to. This was always a mystery to us. Now, instead of reading the list to her, Grandfather returned to the fireplace, sat in his chair, and tore the names into strips. He put them all into his hat and came to the bed, holding it out to her.

"Pick out two," he said. "He needs a double name."

Grandma said names like Ezra Hosea, Moses Aaron, and others flashed through her mind. "Oh, God," she prayed silently, "please guide my hand to the right ones." With a real effort she reached into the hat and handed two slips to Grandfather.

"Jeremiah Taylor," he read aloud. Grandma sighed in relief. "Jeremiah Taylor Cherry sounds fine for a Methodist minister." Wholly spent, she went to sleep to dream of her firstborn standing tall and straight in the pulpit.

Papa said that one of his earliest memories was the whirr of the spinning wheel and the thump of the loom as Grandma and Aunt Jane made the cloth for their clothes. Grandfather raised flax and cotton, and sheep furnished the wool. Most of the clothes were woven of cotton or linen and wool, "linsey-woolsey," a material from which the shifts were made.

Shifts were the only clothes little boys wore until they got past frying size and got their first pair of homespun pants. The shifts hung loosely from the shoulders past the knees. As a shift was outgrown it was passed down to the next in size, and the younger boys seldom had a new garment.

As each boy reached the age when he could follow his father into the field, he was given a small hoe, handmade by Grandfather, so he could work along with him. At the age of ten, a boy was expected to be able to plow a straight furrow behind a mule.

They were not exempted from helping in the house, either. Stovewood had to be chopped and kept piled handy on the front porch and back stoop, and wash days found one of them down by the spring filling the big wash kettle, making a fire, and rubbing the clothes in the first tub.

In the dead of winter when there was little to do on the farm, a wandering teacher came to the little schoolhouse and taught two or three months. The parents of the children took turns boarding him, which was part of his pay.

The schools were built of hand-hewn logs by the parents in each neighborhood. The windows were small, and on dark days it was hard to see. The benches and desks were split logs set up at different heights and a short boy's legs got very tired dangling above the floor. School days were long, too, as long as the light from the sun lasted.

For the most part lunches were brought in tin pails with a tight top. Extra biscuits were baked at breakfast and filled with fried eggs, side meat, or chicken. There were baked sweet potatoes and biscuits with butter and preserves for the children from prosperous families. Those with less had to content themselves with a piece of cornpone or a sweet potato.

Funny incidents have come down through the years. One day as Papa sat in school practicing on his slate, a little boy sitting next to him on the bench (forgetting where he was) yelled out, "He whooped him!"

Papa looked to see where the boy was pointing and saw two lice fighting in the hair of the boy who sat in front of them. Sure enough, one louse had won the battle.

At the outcry, the schoolmaster came running with his hickory switch to administer the usual whaling such things called for. There was no allowance for foolishness in school in those days. Education was a serious business.

The first thing Grandma did when the boys came home from school was sit before the fire and go through their hair with a fine-tooth comb looking for lice. Papa said he could still hear the pop one made as Grandma tossed it into the fire where it exploded.

Papa craved knowledge as most boys craved food. Somewhere he got three books, a Bible, *Pilgrim's Progress*, and the *Blue Backed Speller*. He cherished the books and often read from them to his younger brothers, who also had a thirst for "book learning." As Grandfather read from the Bible in the evenings by the fireside, Papa listened to the words. A desire to know more about them filled his mind and never left.

Papa was nine when the Civil War started. He heard his father and mother talking about it. The Cherry family was divided on the issue, and Grandmother wept when one of Papa's favorite cousins came to say goodbye as he left for the Confederate Army. This cousin's brother had joined the Union Army. Both were killed at the Battle of Bull Run, fighting on opposite sides.

Papa said he could remember how both his parents sobbed the night when they heard the news. "War is an instrument of the devil," Grandfather Cherry told his sons. "Maybe this will be the last one you will know about."

Grandfather sold supplies to the Union Army during the war. Papa went with him one day to deliver them. It was necessary to have a pass to go over a bridge and enter the army camp, and Papa had heard dreadful tales about what happened to those who didn't have one. He wasn't sure that his father had one, either, so as they approached the bridge in the ox cart and saw the soldier stationed there with his musket, the "Halt!" which rang out into the air set Papa to trembling. But fear was something that the Cherry brothers had been drilled to ignore, so he sat up very straight on the wagon seat, determined to hide his feelings.

It was with real relief that Papa saw his father pull the pass out of his pocket and hand it to the guard. Now they would not be thrown into some foul prison. Relief must have shown on his face, for the soldier turned aside to hide his grin as Grandfather drove the wagon across the bridge in safety.

Canmera Circuit

THE farms of my two grandfathers were on opposite sides of Barren River. During the Civil War they were on opposite sides, too. To Grandfather Cherry, slavery was an unthinkable atrocity. None of his boys were old enough to fight, and he was exempted because of farming. Work to him was an honorable part of life and it was said that he looked down on Grandpa White because he owned slaves and used them to make his way of life easier.

An example of their differences was the way each man got water into the yard. Both had springs running freely in a dip behind the houses, which sat on hills. Grandfather Cherry saw to it that the water was carried for the most part by his boys, but carried by hand. Grandpa White used an invention of his fathers, a crude kind of turbine. He built a dam in the stream and forced water through a pipe up into the yard.

"Anybody too lazy to tote a bucket of water . . . ." Grandfather Cherry stopped there in disgust; meanwhile, Grandpa White sat under a shade tree and thought up ways to make money and do things without such hard work. He took up trading as his father and grandfather had before him, and went to far away farms, buying or trading for their produce:

hams, molasses, lard, livestock, and so on. These he sold on a commission basis to captains of river boats towing rafts or barges to the larger towns either up or downstream.

Grandfather Cherry could never understand how Grandpa White, with his shiftless ways, could have so much more of the world's goods than he did.

Mama often told us that her folks never fully decided whether their slaves owned them or the reverse. She said that as children they were afraid of their black Mammy who kept keen switches for disobedient legs. Mammy's word was law in that house.

While Grandfather Cherry's family consisted of all boys, Grandpa White's ran to girls (red-headed at that) for the most part. There were only three boys out of the twelve White children, and young men in the neighborhood had a preference for the Whites' house on Sunday afternoons (which was the established courting time). Because of Grandma White's poor health the girls learned to keep house early, and nowhere were there better managers. It was rumored that nobody in that section could make biscuits like the White sisters.

When Leona Celeste (my mother) was old enough to go with boys, a widower in the community who was well off in worldly goods set his eye on her and everyone began to congratulate her on her good fortune. The only drawback was young Jeremiah Taylor Cherry ("Jerry") whose blue eyes held promise of more than material things. Her advisors tried to point out to her what an easy time she would have in a nice home, already built and furnished. The age difference wasn't so bad. What was twenty years?

Take that Jerry, now. His father would give him a small farm with a run-down cabin when he married. His salary as a teacher wasn't much, and since he planned to be a preacher, think what a preacher's wife faced! Handed-down clothes, wondering where the next meal was coming from, to be always watched and criticized by the public, moving every year or so.

"Think, Lestie, think!"

And think Mama did—but not about the widower, but of Jerry and the excitement in his smile.

On February 29, 1876, Papa and Mama were married at Grandfather White's home near Woodbury, Kentucky. An uncle, Wesley Hudnall, who was a Unitarian minister, performed the ceremony.

They tell the story on Papa that, since he didn't want to seem too anxious, he delayed his trip for two hours and was late for the wedding. He was riding on horseback since the February roads were too muddy for a buggy.

My parents spent the first few months of married life at Grandfather Cherry's house, where Lestie became from then on the favorite sister-in-law of all the boys. Mama often said that if she had ever known a saint on earth it was Grandma Martha Stahl Cherry. "I never heard her say anything bad about anybody in my life."

Later the couple moved to a cabin on the Old Maxey Place. Grandfather had given it to them, along with some acreage, a few hens, a cow, a sow expecting pigs, and a mule. There Papa farmed in summer, taught school three months in winter, and studied every minute he could to prepare for the ministry.

Here in the Maxey cabin the first three children were born, all boys. Mama said each time she was pregnant Papa wished for a girl. He always distrusted the motives of the male sex, and he showed this by his severe discipline of the boys. He followed the example of Grandfather Cherry, whose punishment was seldom or never laced with mercy. He pointed out that all his brothers had turned out fine under that regime.

After his years of study Papa finally got an appointment to preach at Canmera. He was thirty. He was excited over his first pastorate. He sold the farm and put the money away to buy a place later when he and Mama retired. No matter how badly that money was needed in the years of poverty and illness, it was never touched until he bought ten acres near Elkton.

Mama's first experience as a minister's wife came in the move to Canmera. She learned after that to take food enough along for several days, but this time she packed most of it in wagons which were to follow the one she and Papa were in. She felt grateful for all the good things the relatives and friends had given them. She was sure the loaded wagons would arrive at the same time they did.

Instead, the one-horse spring wagon in which they were traveling arrived in Canmera late Saturday night. Later they learned the heavier wagons had been delayed. It was too late to go to a store, and all Mama could find to cook the next day were four Irish potatoes which the former minister had left. She put the potatoes into the ashes while the boys stood around impatiently waiting for food. Just as they were done, a knock came on the door. There stood four children.

Mama was busily dividing the potatoes between the boys when Papa, not realizing her dilemma, said heartily, "Give our visitors some, too."

34

"How I hated to share those potatoes," Mama confessed in later years when she told the story to me. "I looked at those children and thought of the Sunday dinner they must have enjoyed, and begrudged them every bite they ate."

After the visitors left, Mama began to look around more closely at the "fully furnished parsonage" they had been promised as an inducement for accepting this church. The night before she had put the sleepy little boys into beds with sagging springs and mattresses. Not too clean, either, she noticed. There were a few chairs here and there, some with rounds missing. The floors were bare except for the front room in which someone's discarded faded carpet covered part of the splintery floor. A rickety sofa stood in front of one bare window.

In the kitchen she found a cracked step stove, a table covered with worn oilcloth, a few straight chairs, and a pie safe. Mama said she was thankful for the nice things following, like featherbeds Aunt Jane had helped her make from down they had plucked from Grandma's geese. The hard mattresses would be softened by them and her pretty quilts would help lighten the drab bedrooms.

Since the move was in October, it wasn't long before Mama got her first taste of the Thanksgiving missionary offering. Most of it was used clothing out of the missionary barrel which more prosperous churches sent to the poorer ones as part of their home missions projects. There was little in the barrel she could use. She was pregnant, tired, and discouraged. Papa, seeing how she felt, found a young girl to help out, and Mama was delighted. Canmera was predominantly Catholic, and when Mama found out that the girl was Catholic, too, she assured Papa (who distrusted anyone who was not Methodist) that the boys were too young to be hurt by the "pagan" influence.

The girl loved the boys dearly, and worried because they had never been baptized by a priest. So, one day when Papa and Mama were visiting, she called her own priest to come to the house and baptize them, paying him out of her own small wages.

Mama heard about it first from the oldest boy. She feared Papa's wrath when he heard, but all he said was, "It didn't do any harm, and her motives were good. Ignorance has to be overlooked sometimes. I'll have to convert her."

But in spite of all Papa's teaching, the girl remained a staunch Catholic.

One time when I got older and Mama and I talked of Canmera, I asked Mama if she ever thought about the warnings she had had about being a preacher's wife.

"I'm afraid I did," she told me. She smiled, and a faraway look crossed her face. "It wasn't always easy. Living with Papa might be hard, but there were few dull times."

5

A Swollen Creek

THE spring of 1888 was as changeable as the winter before it had been—bad weather for sore throats and lung fever. Papa, being a family man, enjoyed taking one of the children with him on appointments. For several months he had been unable to do this because of the weather. Finally, a Saturday dawned bright and clear, with the sun shining as though it had never rained or snowed. Papa was due to leave for his country church and he said to Mama, "It's so pretty out, maybe I'll take Roxy with me. She hasn't been out for a long time now, and we'll be back early tomorrow afternoon."

Mama knew that Roxy, the first girl to follow three husky boys, was Papa's special delight. Papa had told her how the child, riding along in the squeaky buggy behind the hired horse, loved to talk with him and hear the songs brought over from the old country and handed down to the family. Her favorite was:

Wind in the clover,
Ride up to Dover,
Sour meat, sweet meat,
Wind in the clover.

She always asked, "Papa, how can clover ride up to Dover on the wind?" But she often told Mama, "Papa knows everything."

Papa was still waiting for Mama's decision, and as she looked at his anxious face she reluctantly consented.

"Roxy hasn't been feeling too peart lately, but wrap her up good, Papa, and I think she'll be all right."

Roxy didn't say much on the long trip across the country roads. Most of the time she leaned on Papa's arm and dozed, even when they came to the creek which had to be forded, a venture that had always thrilled her. It had begun to rain by the time they arrived at the Smiths' where they were to stay. She wasn't hungry at supper time, refusing the jam she always chose at this house. Papa felt her cheek; her face was flushed. "She must have a little fever," he worried. "Is your throat sore, Roxy?" he asked. She nodded and Papa mixed up his remedy for colds and sore throats: turpentine in melted lard, soaked into a flannel rag, heated and wrapped around the neck.

"Please, Papa, don't. It burns." In telling about it later on, Papa said he wished he had listened to her, but no matter how uncomfortable the remedy, it was all they had, and must be used.

Roxy began to choke about midnight. The man of the house came to Papa and said, "The rain is coming down harder, and the creek will rise. I'd better go for a doctor while I can." Not that a doctor had ever been able to do much in cases like Roxy's, but every straw was grasped when this kind of sore throat hit a loved one.

"Tell Mrs. Cherry to come with the doctor, too," Papa told the man.

Quickly the child's choking became agonized. "Water," Roxy begged, but when it was brought to her in a glass, and she tried to swallow, it ran from her mouth. She reached her small hand into the glass, trying to suck it from her fingers, only to choke worse.

Papa walked the floor, the child in his arms. Too many times that winter he had been called into the homes of others and had held their children over his shoulder. This time it was his child who was making those same choking sounds he'd heard too often before. He had sat with families through it all, until the crisis passed, which it seldom did. Most times death brought relief from the suffering. Papa thought of the words of comfort he'd tried to offer then, but they didn't seem the right ones now, just empty mouthings.

The rain poured down, and the creek roared with the filling of debris the deluge was dumping into its banks. Would morning never come? Papa thought. Could Mama get there in time?

Daylight, grayed by heavy clouds, began to streak the sky. He could see through the window the buggy with Mama and the doctor standing across the swollen creek. Mama, disregarding the mud, jumped down from the buggy and ran to the bank, separated from her child by surging logs and trash that filled the creek bed. There could be no crossing until the creek went down in its own time.

Papa walked to the window. "See, Roxy, there's Mama." Maybe the sight of Mama would work a miracle. Roxy made an effort to look, then a fit of choking came and she lay quiet on Papa's shoulder. Her struggle was over.

Papa laid her down and went to the creek bank. No

sound could have been heard above the roar of the water, but Mama needed no words to tell her that her first girl child was gone, without the comfort of her mother's arms. A kind of bitterness crept into her heart, she told someone later, bitterness against Papa, who had taken Roxy away when she wasn't feeling well, bitterness against herself for allowing it, and bitterness against God who had let them down, returning small thanks for all the times Papa had gone in the middle of the night to try to bring comfort to those who were burdened as they were now.

Standing on the wet creek bank, Mama felt the strong movement of the child she now carried. She hoped it would be another girl. Papa had already picked out a name, Nellie Grace, and grace it would take to carry on.

It was several hours before the creek went down enough to ford, but when Mama stood over her child, wet to the knees, her face streaked with mud and tears, the bitterness vanished. Pity took its place as she looked at Papa, exhausted from his long night's vigil. He lay in a light sleep on the couch, his fingers twitching as if eager to do something to help Roxy. Mama touched his face gently with a fingertip, and went quietly by the fire to dry her muddy clothes until the creek lowered enough for them to take Roxy back home to the burying ground. She could hear the tapping of the hammer as their host made Roxy's small wooden coffin.

As they sat side by side on the wagon seat, with the hastily built box holding the body of their child, Papa said, "She won't be alone, Mama; there have been so many graves before hers this winter."

"I wonder if the doctors will ever find a cure for

membraneous croup [diphtheria]?" Mama's voice was doubtful, and she thought of the five other small ones at home. Once again she felt the stir of the new life near her heart. Funny how each child became someone special, filling a need in the family's lives. Roxy had held her own place and always would. (The older girls told later how each year, at spring cleaning time, Mama took out Roxy's best dress, aired it, and showed it to the others.)

And each time Papa preached a funeral, he spoke from a heart that had shared the same hurt as those whom he tried to comfort.

6

A Yard of Roses

IN many places in Kentucky there were swampy areas, and everyone who lived in them dreaded summer and fall chills, which were blamed on the dampness and night air. Typhoid also struck, sometimes in epidemic proportions, but it was not until 1880 that the disease was found to be caused by a germ.

My sister Mary, the oldest girl, was recovering from typhoid at the time of a move from Jeffersonville to Brandenburg, so Papa sent the rest of the family ahead to the new appointment and stayed behind to nurse her until she was well enough to move. When she was, he put her on a cot and brought her by boat to the new parsonage. Mary was thin from the starvation diet which typhoid patients were given then, and as she lay on the deck on her cot, the captain of the boat came by. "Bring her a tray of food," he bellowed to the crew. "This child is starving!"

An enormous tray was brought to Mary, heaped with all kinds of food. She reached for it eagerly, and Papa fed her bits from it, making sure she ate nothing that might hurt her. He had known too many patients on their way to recovery from typhoid who overate after days of fasting and died from the excess. So Mary's voracious appetite was ignored. Those who lived through a bout with the disease remembered the terrible hunger while convalescing the worst part of all.

The next summer, Mama was getting over an illness and was pregnant, as usual. Mary and David Ella were distressed over her condition and wanted to do something special for her. For a long time they had been saving Arbuckle coffee coupons. Their hearts were set on a picture called "A Yard of Roses." There were other selections offered, too, such as "A Yard of Pansies" and "A Yard of Chickens," but since the rose was Mama's favorite flower, "A Yard of Roses" was their choice. The picture really was a yard long, and they talked about how pretty it would be over the mantel.

Mama was so weak, they decided, that the picture might bring new life to her, so they must not wait any longer. They got a big girl in the fourth grade to write a letter for them to the company. They knew they were supposed to send seventeen coupons and seventeen cents for the offer, they explained, but their mother was very sick and they were sure the picture would cheer her up. So they were sending thirteen cents and thirteen coupons, which were all they had been able to save. They promised to send the rest as soon as they were able to get them. They hoped the Arbuckle Company would trust them.

They waited impatiently. Then one day a letter came from the company telling them not to send the extra four coupons and four cents. The "Yard of Roses" was in the mail. The girls were elated. When it arrived, they spent a long time admiring it.

Papa always made improvements wherever he lived, and in Bradenburg he was having the church doors changed. There had been two at the front, one for the women and small children and one for the men and older boys. Papa liked to see families sitting together, so he was having one door built in the center to replace the two. Mary and David had made friends with the carpenters. They often visited them and were allowed to take the long spiral strips that came off the wood when planing to pretend they had curly hair. Eager to share their surprise with someone, they took it to the church and showed it to the men.

One of the carpenters remembered that he had seen an old picture in the basement. "How would you like to have a frame for your 'Yard of Roses'?" he asked them.

The girls were almost overcome. They couldn't believe their good fortune, but they kept it a secret from Mama and the rest of the family until the proud day when they presented it to her. It was a prized possession and is still in the family.

For the rest of their lives, Mary and David claimed that Mama's miraculous recovery began when they gave her "A Yard of Roses." And everywhere Mama moved, she could always enjoy roses, her favorite flower, however bare of blossoms her own yard might be.

7

Party Dress

TIMES were desperate when the three oldest Cherry girls were almost grown. Try as she could, Mama could only furnish one best dress between them. The answer to that, of course, was letting only one girl at a time accept a party invitation. Fortunately, the girls were the same height and Mama had made the dress rather loose in the middle to allow for the varying dimensions of their waists. Mary pulled the waist tight with a sash, David had to let it out a bit more, and Nell an inch or two further. This, of course, necessitated ironing out the creases each time it was worn. To do this, the iron was wiped clean, heated, then tested with spit on the end of a finger until it sizzled just right for smoothing without scorching.

This night it was David's turn to go to the party. She opened the wardrobe door and took out the dress which swung from its homemade hanger. In honor of the dress the girls had wrapped the piece of wooden lathe with shiny cloth and added a length of hair ribbon (slightly worn from use, it was true, but still a bit more fitting for a festive gown than the ordinary string that centered the paper-wrapped hangers).

Carefully David shook out the folds and ran a hand lovingly over the soft fabric. She smoothed the lace collar which had been removed from one of Mama's best dresses. The lace was wearing thin, she noticed, and the sash showed breaks in its silky length.

When David was almost ready to go, she stood before the mirror brushing her long auburn hair, trying new ways to dress it. She thought of the time and effort it had taken to persuade Papa to let her attend the party. It always required some doing and she hoped she might be spared the inevitable lecture.

"Vanity, vanity, all is vanity!" In the mirror she saw Papa's reflection as he stood in the doorway, and fear began to build as he lectured her on his chosen Scripture. There had been times in the past when Papa, persuaded by his own oration, had decided one of his daughters could not go out and face the temptations of the secular world. David was afraid this might be another such occasion.

Hastily, to prove that she was not vain, David put her hair up in the pompadour style popular at the time, slipped the dress over her head, fastened the sash, and turned to go.

For a minute Papa barred her way through the door; it was then that Mama's voice called from the kitchen.

"Papa, I can't lift this pot off the stove."

Papa turned to go to the kitchen and David slipped through the door, thankful to hear the knock that announced the arrival of her escort for the night. She would be careful, no matter how much fun she was having, to get home by nine-thirty, or they might meet Papa coming to bring her home.

She felt a surge of gratitude to Mama, for she knew Mama would find other chores at the back of the house for Papa to do until she and her beau could start their walk to the party.

Mama had a way of coming through in a pinch.

Ithiel

IN the spring and summer of 1898, slogans reading "Remember the Maine" were posted everywhere. An outrage had been committed against our government, and every man, woman, and child was filled with righteous indignation. An expeditionary force was being assembled from volunteers to assault Santiago by land.

Ithiel was one of the first to volunteer. The day he left Mama was filled with a mixture of pride and sadness as she moved about, pregnant as usual, fixing a lunch for him to eat aboard the train.

Letters came from Ithiel at the camp, enthusiastic ones about the excitement of a trip to Cuba, but always at the end he wrote, "I miss your cooking, Mama, especially your ham biscuits."

One day a letter came:

"We'll be passing through town next Friday on the troop train. Please be at the station to see me."

It took two days to bake the cakes, boil the ham, and get ready the foods that Ithiel especially liked.

Mama forgot her swollen feet and aching back in her labor of love. "At least I can do that for him," she comforted herself.

Mama packed the food into a huge split-oak basket strong enough to withstand rough handling, covered it with a clean flour sack towel, and fastened the top. Papa, as usual, took the family to the station long before train time—he was never known to be late anywhere. It seemed ages to them before the train whistle sounded far up the track. A long line of cars filled with soldiers slowed, then stopped. Anxious eyes scanned the faces, but Ithiel was not there.

Papa approached the conductor. "Will there be any more trains?"

The conductor nodded. "Two." Tired and harassed by the noisy young men in his care, his answer was curt.

As the first train pulled out, another whistle sounded and a second engine and a line of cars came to a stop. Mama looked carefully for Ithiel. He wasn't on the second train and it soon moved on. Mama was getting anxious.

"There's another one." Papa's knuckles were white as he clutched the basket of food. "Ithiel will have to be on that one."

The wait between trains was longer this time. Mama's feet were almost swollen out of her shoes from standing so long. They always swelled before each baby was born. As she waited, Mama thought of Ithiel as a baby, her first son, and of his tenderness to her.

She remembered the summer when she couldn't seem to get well from her latest lying in. The ice which had been cut in the winter and put into ice houses had melted long since. People were afraid, anyhow, this late in the season, to scramble around in the sawdust to find a piece of ice, for it was said that snakes liked the coolness of the storage pit's bottom.

Ithiel had come to the bed, offering her a drink from the cistern, tepid and tasteless. "I think I'd get well if I had just once piece of ice," Mama told him.

Half an hour later he came back into the room holding out a small dripping package. "I got it out of the bottom of the icehouse," he told her. Mama ignored the bit of clinging sawdust and put the ice to her lips greedily.

There were so many other memories of Ithiel—one about the time they had just moved to another circuit and hadn't had a chance to clean up outside.

Church was over and dinner had been served. The older and younger members of the house were napping. Something roused Papa from his sleep and he went into the yard. Ithiel was working diligently moving rubbish into a corner: cans, broken bottles, wire, and bits of wood.

"What are you doing?" Papa roared. (Papa thought that roaring added emphasis to his words, and many a parishioner had been startled from a furtive nap by the volume of Papa's voice.)

Ithiel turned a dirt-streaked face toward his father, extending his small dirty hand for emphasis, as he had seen Papa do.

"You said this morning that hell was an ugly place. I'm making hell!"

As Mama tiredly waited for the third train to come, she remembered how her son had made hell in the backyard. The pile of ugliness he had made compared well, she thought, with the hell which war made.

The whistle sounded at last, loud and clear, and the roar of the train was shattering as it raced down the track. But something was wrong. It wasn't slowing down. Young faces, far too young for war, flashed by. Three cars passed, then the fourth. There was Ithiel, almost at the end of the last car!

Forgetting her exhaustion, Mama grabbed the heavy basket of food from Papa and ran along the side of the train holding it out to Ithiel, but he couldn't reach it. He threw her a kiss, and she saw his lips move but his words were lost in the roar of the speeding train.

Mama dropped the basket on the platform and sat down on it, ignoring her bulky weight. She put her hands over her face and wailed aloud, tears streaming through her fingers.

Papa sought for words to comfort her. "Never mind, Mammy. We can eat the food when we get home."

And for his efforts to comfort Mama, Papa heard one of the few caustic remarks she ever made to him. "*You* eat it!" she said, still crying. "I'd choke!"

Number Ten

FROM December 1876 until November 1893, Mama had given birth to nine children: Ithiel Thaddeus, Ariel Clarence, Zephaniah Taylor, Ulalia Roxanna, Mary Martha, David Ella, Nellie Grace, Elizabeth Elliott, and Katherine Celeste.

When Katherine was born Mama had been so sick that she could not remember the date, so Katherine's actual birthday was always uncertain. The recovery was slow, and when six years passed without another pregnancy Mama began to feel safe at last. She was forty-two, the age most women stopped having babies.

The family had been in Franklin about a month when Mama began to have the telltale symptoms she had experienced nine times before. She was overwhelmed. She thought of the hard times all of them had suffered in poor circuits, where Papa's popularity had been at a low ebb. The rumor was going around in Franklin that he wasn't too well liked here, either. This meant, as always, another move when October came.

"I just can't have another baby," she told Papa. "I'll die if I do. We can't feed the ones we already have the kind of food they need." Mama started to cry, something she seldom did.

Papa was shocked at the news. He, too, had been sure that Katherine would be their last child. "How far along are you?" he asked. "Maybe it's something else," he offered hopefully.

"Just a few weeks," Mama said, wiping her eyes. "But I always know right away," she reminded him.

Papa nodded his head, and ran his hand through his thinning hair worriedly.

"I just can't have another child," Mama repeated. "There is no money for shoes for the other children. The ones they have aren't decent to wear to school, much less to church." Mama started sobbing again.

"You can use the leftovers from Katherine," Papa offered hopefully. He was pacing the floor now, upset by Mama's emotional outburst.

"*What* leftovers?" Mama asked. "I gave them all away. There's not even a diaper left. I just can't face it." Mama dried her eyes and said, "There's a new doctor in town. Maybe he knows some way."

"Maybe he does," Papa said.

Mama was relieved, for she hadn't known what his reaction would be. Papa had welcomed each baby, especially the girls, and girls it had been the last six times.

Encouraged, Mama said, "Will you ask him to stop by?" Papa didn't answer, but he put on his hat and went out the door.

When Dr. Smith came, he listened to Mama sympathetically. As he got up to leave, he laid an arm across Mama's drooping shoulders. He set a small bottle on her bedside table and said as he turned to go,

"You can take this if you really don't want another baby."

Papa had observed the whole scene in silence, a troubled look on his face.

Mama turned to him now. "What do you think, Papa?" she asked.

"It's your decision, Lestie. Whatever you decide . . . ." How like Papa, Mama thought, to leave her alone with this problem!

All that night Mama walked the floor quietly so she wouldn't disturb Papa, sleeping peacefully through the night. Many times she picked up the bottle, holding it in her hand. Once she pulled the cork and put it to her lips. The taste was bitter. She put the bottle back on the table, sat in Papa's big chair, and covered her face with her hands. Tears ran through her fingers, washing away her fears.

When dawn began to fill the sky, Mama went outside. She opened the bottle with a steady hand and poured its contents into the trash barrel.

"Even if I don't have one diaper," she told herself, "I just can't do it."

David, the seamstress in the family, helped Mama make as many clothes as they could out of anything they had, but still the layette was inadequate.

A few weeks before I was born Papa preached at the funeral of a stillborn baby. The child resembled a beautiful wax doll as it lay, dressed in expensive handmade clothes, in a casket lined with lace. Mama felt a surge of bitterness as she compared the few things she and David had accumulated with this baby's lovely things which would never be used. Sometimes life just was not fair.

After the funeral my parents went to see the young mother. As Mama, awkward in her bulk, came into the room where she lay in bed, the young mother's eyes filled with tears. "You have so many children." A deep sadness filled her voice. "I've lost my only one."

The next day Mama heard a knock on the door. The father of the dead child stood on the porch, a large box in his hand. "My wife wants you to have these baby clothes, Sister Cherry." Before Mama could find a passage for words through her throat, which was tightened with emotion, he turned quickly and left.

My birth was a hard one. The doctor called me a blue baby, and in 1899 blue babies were not expected to live over two years, so as soon as Mama was able to go to the church she dressed me carefully in the most beautiful clothes that had been given to her. For a moment she felt a rush of sadness that all her other children had not been so well dressed for their christenings.

My sisters told me in later years that Mama's and Papa's faces were glowing with pride as Papa took me into his arms, dipped his hand into the fount, and placed it on my head. "I baptize you, Frances Willard, in the name of the Father, the Son, and the Holy Ghost."

I was a little over two months old when I made my first move: to Trenton, where Papa later offended some church members. We moved again the following October to the Elkton circuit, where Papa pastored three country churches. We lived in a small house in town. Mama's health was still very poor and Papa hired Mobile, a teen-age girl, to care for me, since my older sisters were in school all day and couldn't help. Papa never allowed anything to keep his children out of school.

The first actual memory I have is one of a smoky fireplace and the feel of Mobile's soft brown arms as she sat in a squeaky rocker and sang "Minstrel Man" to me. I was coughing hard and at intervals Mobile dipped up the syrup oozing from an onion covered with brown sugar as it warmed before the open fire, and gave it to me in a spoon. It soothed my throat and made me sleepy. The soft moaning sound of Mobile's singing came back to me in later years when wind sighing in tall pines on Lake Michigan's shores brought back the haunting music.

Our house was close to the public town square. There was a big courthouse in the center, a place I was never tempted to visit because of its awesome size. I can remember running away to town, one time in the rain with Papa's big umbrella, which he had left open to drain on the porch, behind me. It was summertime and Mobile had gone by then. My sister Mary had been given charge over me. Either she or one of my other sisters always caught me before I could explore the second side of the square. One place I avoided: the barber shop. The name sounded scary to me. I pictured the barber as a big black bear, and when Papa decided to take me there to get a haircut, he didn't understand the screaming tantrum I threw. Not until my sister Mary took me on her lap and questioned me did the real reason for my fear come out.

I must have gotten away with a lot of bad behavior about then, for the doctor had told my folks that I had a leaky valve in my heart and I must not be "crossed." The older girls were ordered never to tease me or get me upset, and for the most part they didn't, except on the few occasions when I was left completely in their care. Then they released a little of their frustration with my onerous ways by a surreptitious pinch or slap.

Elkton was the site of Vanderbilt Training School, which was especially set up for the training of candidates for the ministry who would attend Vanderbilt University in Nashville, Tennessee. Mama kept two students and the board money they paid helped keep the family in food.

From the small house in town we moved to the country.

10

And Turnips Filled the Barn

THE first year we lived in the country parsonage near Elkton was a full one for all of us. The older girls continued to go to Vanderbilt Training School and I reveled in the open spaces around our house and the country atmosphere. Papa had a garden and bought a cow, which we named Becky. Nell was given the task of doing the milking, and the cow became attached to her. The pasture was bordered by the lane that went by our house, and one day when Nell's current boyfriend walked home from school with her, Becky recognized her from across the field where she was grazing. With a happy bellow, Becky loped over to greet Nell with continuous delighted moos. Nell was humiliated, for she had kept her chore a secret from her friends, who had no such plebeian work assigned to them. Nell's face was the color of the red clay in the lane when she and her boyfriend opened the gate and came into the yard. I had observed the incident from the front porch so I asked Nell, "Why didn't you pet Becky? You always do."

Nell's boyfriend laughed, which made Nell say a short "Goodbye," and go into the house, slamming the door.

This was the year, too, that Grandfather White came to visit us. He looked like the picture of Santa Claus with his white hair and beard and his twinkling blue eyes. He was popular with all the grandchildren, and we always argued over which family he would visit next.

It was Grandfather White who taught me to walk again after something happened to my legs and they forgot how to move. I awakened one night with a vague memory of having fallen off our front porch while Nell was serenading Becky with a zither to see if she liked music. I found the whole family and the doctor standing around my bed. The doctor felt my legs. "Can you feel this?" he asked me.

I shook my head. I wondered why everyone was crying. I didn't hurt at all.

After I began to get better, Grandfather White would carry me outside, set me in the sun against the trunk of the big oak tree, and rub my legs for a long time. He held me up, and as my legs got stronger, he propped me against the tree and held out his arms as if I were a toddler. He begged me to come to him, and everyone in the family rejoiced the day I took my first step.

About that time Becky went dry and every morning Mama had to walk to a neighbor's house where there was a new baby and wash its clothes in exchange for a pint of milk for me. With love like that I had to get well.

As fall approached, Papa began to see about getting ready for cold weather.

Early fall was one of the times when church members brought their quarterly dues. Most of them were farmers and their offering was made up of produce they raised. There was flour, meal, meat in season, vegetables, chickens. Most of the offerings were welcome, but that year there had been an early drought which prevented most vegetables from maturing. A tardy rain, however, brought on an abundance of late turnips.

Mama always watched anxiously at each quarterage time to see what there would be to put on the table. She was a wonderful cook and, given any kind of decent food, she fed us well. This fall, every time a wagon or buggy drove into the yard, she met it with Papa. Each time the church member set a tow bag on the ground, we got so we could almost say along with him, "Brother Cherry, my crops didn't do much this year, so I wondered if you could use a bushel of turnips." The turnips seemed to fill the barn.

Several times Mama protested with Papa. "Why don't you tell your members to bring something else?"

Papa would scratch his head and say soothingly, "Now, Mammy, if that's all they have, we must take them."

So turnips it was that year, turnips on the table three times a day, it seemed to me. How good a potato would have tasted!

11

Zeph and the Rainy Day

THAT same year when we lived in the country parsonage near Elkton, Zeph, the youngest of my three older brothers, was still at home. When he walked across the big front yard on his hands or rode me piggyback, loping, I was ecstatic. He was so good looking, more like Papa than any of the other boys. Zeph was tall, lean like Papa, almost to emaciation, and his eyes darted the same lightning flashes that Papa's did when he was aroused. Only his voice, deep though it was, never roared and thundered like Papa's. Zeph's tone was always gentle. "Thunder from Mount Sinai" was one of Papa's own expressions, and it didn't take much imagination on our part to know what the thunder sounded like. After watching a session between Papa and Zeph when my brother had committed some misdemeanor, it was hard to believe that the same father who was so hard on Zeph also took me into his big armchair every day and sang me to sleep.

One day had been a particularly bad one between Papa and Zeph. That night Zeph ate very little supper before he went silently to the back room where he slept. Mama's face had a troubled look as she and Papa went to bed. From my trundle bed beside theirs I could hear her stirring long after Papa's steady snore proclaimed his depth of slumber. I couldn't sleep either, but when I started to complain to Mama, her hand closed softly over my mouth, and in the light of the full moon shining in the window I saw her shake her head. It was then that I heard soft steps in the kitchen. Mama crept from her side of the bed and went out of the room in her bare feet. Careful not to make any noise, I slid out of bed, too, and followed her, peeping around the kitchen door. Zeph stood there fully dressed. On the table lay a small bundle wrapped in a towel. The end of a sock hung out, so I supposed it must be Zeph's clothes.

Tears were running down Mama's face, and Zeph laid an arm across her shoulders. I couldn't hear what it was he whispered, but Mama kissed him gently and went to the pie safe. She reached into the back and brought out a Mason jar. She unscrewed the top and eased its contents onto a dishcloth, pennies for the most part, but also nickles and dimes and a few quarters. As she handed him the money, Zeph, forgetting to be quiet, said, "But Mama, it's your butter and egg money! You've saved it for years!"

Mama again put her finger to her lips, gesturing for silence, as she glanced toward the door leading to the bedroom. She took Zeph into her arms for a moment before he went out the back door.

I wasn't quick enough to get back into bed before Mama came into the bedroom. When she saw me, she led me back into the kitchen and whispered to me. It was the only time in my life I ever heard her hint to any of us that we should keep something from Papa.

"Don't tell Papa, Willard. You must not tell." Then to herself, "All I had to give him was $9.56."

Next morning the family was at breakfast when I came into the kitchen. Even in my half-aware state between sleeping and waking I knew that something was wrong. Zeph's place at the table next to mine was vacant, and Papa was in the middle of his usual discourse when one of us was late for a meal. "Now, Mama, where do you suppose that boy can be? I told you he was up to no good. Headstrong young flip! I'll teach him. . . ." Papa's tirade stopped suddenly and he looked at Mama.

"He's gone," Mama told him. There was no lightning in Papa's eyes now. Just the desolation of the after-storm. He spoke in a still, small voice, "Did he take his clothes when he went?"

Mama nodded. I pushed my plate away and began to cry. "I want Zeph," I pleaded, thinking of the fun he had shared with me.

My sisters began to cry, too, but only Mama remained calm.

"I'm sure he will be all right. The other boys got jobs as soon as they left home."

"But he didn't have a cent!" The words straggled out of Papa's throat.

Feeling sorry for Papa, I started to correct him, but Mama shook her head and I remembered my promise in the night. I thought of the time I'd watched Mama count the coins in the jar and asked what she was saving them for. "A rainy day," she said.

Later that afternoon, Mama sat by the window looking out. Not a trace of cheerfulness was in her face now. She was so still. She must have thought she was alone.

I looked out the window, too. The sky was dark, and drops of water spattered the panes of glass.

The rainy day had come.

12

Birth and Death

ALL decent children were protected from facts about birth. A child was not supposed to know that a mama's big stomach was the hiding place for the new sister or brother who mysteriously appeared during a sudden absence, usually while he was visiting a relative or neighbor. I began to notice that when a friend told about being carried to a strange bed away from home in the middle of the night he would also tell of finding a new baby when he got home. I wanted a baby sister or brother so badly that I wished Papa would awaken me in the night and take me away so that I'd find a baby, too.

Mama always "shushed" me when I began to ask why the other children had little sisters or brothers and I didn't. If I really pressed her, she gave me some evasive answer. So I went elsewhere to gain this knowledge and got so many facts that I was completely confused. Some said babies came from tree stumps, some from the doctor's little black bag. Mama finally ordered me to stop asking questions about this, which only made me more curious than ever.

I kept my eyes and ears open. One day I slipped

beneath an open window where Mama and one of her friends were discussing things I wasn't supposed to hear. They used words such as "expecting" and "in the family way" about a woman I knew, and later when she had a baby I knew there was some connection.

I was eagerly listening to hear more when the lady saw me and said to Mama, as she pointed to me, "Little jugs have big ears." Mama sent me away in shame, and I felt my ears, wondering if I were a jug and if my ears were outsized. I never could stand my ears after that!

The same rule didn't hold about death. Papa took me with him to visit the dying ones. I knelt by their bedsides and listened as Papa prayed for their safe passing. It was easy to imagine angels waiting with open arms for some sweet old person who had always been kind.

I was quite young when Papa took me to my first funeral. He sat me down in the front pew (where he could keep an eye on me, I'm sure). First I heard the sound of the mules' feet clomping as they pulled the creaking wagon. They stopped in front of the church. I turned around to see six men dressed in black carrying a rough wooden coffin up the aisle. They set it on two sawhorses which had been placed in front of the pulpit. Papa stood in the aisle waiting, and when I saw the mourners dressed in black with long veils wailing as they came into the church, I was glad he was there. The chief mourner, a tall woman with a veil extending past her waist, supported by two others, led the procession. The women wiped her face and rubbed her hands to comfort her, then ended up wailing along with her. The whole audience began crying too, a little louder every time the mourner said, "Why me?"

When everyone was seated the casket was opened. A man with a hammer pulled out four loose nails and leaned the casket top against the sawhorses. I gasped. the corpse was an old lady, dressed in black. Her mouth gaped open, as if she were trying to breathe, and her eyes were half closed. She seemed to be peeping at me, and I shuddered. I was glad when the service was over, for the combined singing and crying distressed me. It took two men to get the woman away from the corpse as she held onto the body and screamed. When the men put the top back on and nailed it tightly shut this time, the hammer blows reached my heart, and I was not surprised to see the chief mourner faint dead away.

When I got home I asked Mama about the veils and she told me they were carefully kept to be used by any mourner in a neighborhood, and passed around at a time of grief.

While I was at the funeral, I detected a peculiar odor, and decided it was from all the black dresses and suits the people wore. I was glad that Mama didn't wear black like most of the older women (those past thirty) did. Her only concession to the color was the black and white checked aprons she wore over her dresses during the week. For black always had, to me, the smell of death.

13

Nannie

WE had just moved into the tiny parsonage in North Todd County the first time I saw Nannie. I was by the kitchen window making marks on the dusty pane, when Nannie's dark little face appeared at our back door.

"My mammy wants to know if you got anybody to wash for you."

Mama sighed. The house had not been set to rights. Moving boxes and the barrel of dishes were still to be unpacked. "I'd like to know what your mother charges," she said.

Nannie ran down the driveway to our big gate. She undid the latch, jumped on the lowest rail, pushed hard with a bare foot, and circled grandly out into space.

Fascinated, I watched her as she carefully closed the gate and went skipping up the Kentucky clay lane toward her home. In a matter of moments she was back.

"Mammy says will a dollar a week be too much?" she asked my mother. A dollar a week was all right. And that had been the beginning of our friendship.

Nannie was my size, but three years older than I. She made our yard a pleasant place to play. We had huge twin oaks for shade, and the space between them was just right for two girls to lie there facing the sky.

Once Nannie pointed a finger toward scurrying, white clouds. "Anybody with extra eyes can see that one's an angel," she said. And, sure enough, there was a slender cloud that had wings feathering out on each side.

"Extra eyes?" I asked.

Nannie explained that you need extra eyes—an extra nose and ears, too—or you miss a lot of things. Then . . . "Listen!" she said.

I listened hard, but all I could hear was a mockingbird singing.

"Close your eyes and shut your mouth, so you can use all your ears," Nannie whispered.

I squeezed my eyes shut and listened. The music was strangely sweeter now. First it came, loud and joyful, from overhead; but later it drifted down faintly from our pasture hill—or from heaven, maybe.

"Angel music," Nannie whispered.

She showed me toadstools which she said the fairies had planted in the damp earth during the night. If I'd get up and watch in the moonlight, she assured me, I'd see fairies with silver pitchers, putting dew drops on the grass. I never saw them, for sleep always overcame me.

Nannie was patient when I complained about my failure to see fairies. Said she hadn't quite seen them, either. "Maybe we needs to grow bigger, so we can stay awake for a spell."

One afternoon Nannie and I decided to look for a baby.

"Papa calls God the 'All-Seeing Eye,'" I suggested. "Let's ask him to help us."

We had discussed the place where he would live,

and decided Mr. Grumbley's cupola on top of his big barn was God's home. It had four windows, and we didn't know anywhere else you could see in all directions except from that loft. God must live there, we thought. It wasn't too far away, either, just at the end of the lane that ran past our homes. We walked up the road. When we got to the barn we stopped.

"Mr. All-Seeing Eye." Nannie spoke first, since she was the older and wiser of the two. "We ain't up to no mischief. Honest, we ain't. We just want a baby, and we might find one in Mr. Grumbley's stumps." Nannie's dark little face was turned toward the cupola, and I quivered with excitement at being part of the venture.

Encouraged by my playmate's boldness, I started to squeak out our reason. "All-Seeing Eye . . ."

Nannie stopped me with a tiny shake, and her dark eyes looked at me solemnly. She cupped her hand around my ear and whispered, "*Mister* All-Seeing Eye."

My manners corrected, I began again, "Mister All-Seeing Eye, me and Nannie, we are tired of playing with stick dolls. Maybe you could put just one little baby in a stump."

"Yes, sir," Nannie said, when I ran out of words. "We'd keep good care of it for sure."

I clasped Nannie's hand then, and we went toward the woods lot, looking behind us at the four windows, and wondering if the All-Seeing Eye had heard. Once I thought I saw a face in a lower window of the barn, but Nannie scoffed at me, and we decided that the face of the All-Seeing Eye wouldn't have a beard like Mr. Grumbley's.

It was late when we got back home and the low step felt good to two tired little girls.

"Willard," Nannie moved closer to me on the step, and her dark toes began to work in the dust, "I don't reckon the All-Seeing Eye heard us this time. Maybe we been bad a little? Mammy says badness stops up God's ears." She patted my hand and smiled at me.

"I haven't been bad." I thought of the piece of cake I'd left in the food safe, without a single tiny nibble missing. "I *do* want a baby." I began to cry.

Nannie hushed me. "Who's that coming up our lane?"

I strained my eyes to watch, until I could see that it was Mr. Bob from town. People laughed and looked down when they talked about him. They said he embroidered and sewed. When he got to our gate he opened it and came in. We saw that he had a bundle in his arms.

Nannie pulled me up and we stood politely. "Call your ma," she said to me.

"Never mind," Mr. Bob said. "I came to see you." He sat on the step above and opened his bundle.

I caught my breath, and I could hear Nannie's rough sigh. He handed us two rag dolls with yarn hair, dressed like real babies in long clothes. Nannie's was brown like her and mine was made of a white stocking.

I hugged my baby close and whispered to Nannie, almost afraid to speak for fear the dream would end. I felt my heart beat with the rhythm of all mothers when their firstborn is laid in their arms.

"It's so, Nannie?" Nannie nudged me with her free hand.

"Sure, it's so, Willard. Thank the nice gentleman for giving you that baby." Her words brought me back to earth, and when I looked at Mr. Bob to thank him I thought I saw tears in his eyes. I must have been mistaken, though, because Papa said it made folks happy to do nice things.

"Thank you, sir," Nannie said.

Mr. Bob didn't seem to be answering us. He sounded like he was talking to himself. "I'm glad I overheard Mr. Grumbley joking—glad I made the dolls." He stopped and said goodbye, and Nannie and I held our breath until the early night that filled the lane hid him from sight.

The whole earth was hushed, it seemed, listening to our wonder at the babies that nestled in our arms. Gently Nannie began to rock back and forth and chant to herself, her joy too deep to share even with her closest friend.

"Thank you, All-Seeing Eye, for my baby. I'll treat her good and teach her manners." I noticed that Nannie had forgotten to say "Mr.," but I decided that God could take no offense at the way she gentled his name.

The days were too short that summer for Nannie and me as we played with our babies. We took hours deciding on their names. When I heard Mama singing, "His grace is enough for me" as she went about her work, I named my baby "Grace."

Nannie took her name "Charity" from a word I'd heard in one of Papa's texts. "Faith, Hope, and Charity, these three, and the greatest of these is Charity."

I didn't like the way Mama and Papa took to staring at my baby toward the end of the summer, and the looks they gave each other when they did. I talked to Nannie about it, and she said they might be studying, like grown folks sometimes do, the dirt on our dolls, instead of the softness and love underneath.

When I heard Papa tell Mama I'd have to throw my doll away, I ran to Nannie, frantic with fear about my child.

"She does not have germs," I sobbed. "She does not!"

"We better talk to the All-Seeing Eye again," Nannie said.

So we walked to Mr. Grumbley's barn again, more trustful of God now, since he'd brought us our babies.

"Mr. All-Seeing Eye," Nannie said politely, she stopped and scratched her head. "We do have a problem. Seems like it's your problem, too, You give us our babies." Nannie pointed her finger at me. "Her Ma and Pa done said they're going to get rid of her baby. We don't want her baby took away." This time I knew I heard a movement in the barn and when I told Nannie, her eyes got big and shiny.

"Maybe you did, Willard, and maybe we can help the All-Seeing Eye out, too." She thought a minute, then whispered, "Might be a good idea to hide Grace Baby awhile, like Mammy said they hid baby Moses. We can play with her when your folks ain't looking."

Nannie looked back at the cupola and lowered her voice so it couldn't reach the windows.

"Not that I don't trust the All-Seeing Eye," she assured me. "Didn't he bring us our babies?"

We found a cozy place for my doll behind a box in the smokehouse that stood out a little way from the wall. We put fresh hay in and laid Grace Baby on its softness.

That night at supper we heard a knock at the door. Mr. Grumbley stood there with a box in his hand.

"I brought your daughter a rabbit," he said to Papa. Papa looked from Mama to me, then nodded his head and took the box.

"I guess she can have it, under the circumstances."

We went to the smokehouse and put the rabbit inside. I was happy to think that Grace Baby would have company that night.

Next day when I opened the smokehouse door to show Nannie my new pet, it was nowhere to be found.

"Let's get my baby and play," I said. We went to the place we'd hidden her behind the box, and there lay the rabbit, in a mound of cotton. My baby was gone.

"She's gone, she's gone," I wailed, and Papa came running to the smokehouse. He put his arm across my shoulders. Then he stooped down and moved the cotton, and Nannie and I could see six pink baby rabbits nestling close to their mother.

Papa pulled out a piece of cloth from underneath and held it up. Grace Baby's face stared at me from its flat surface, my baby no more, just a piece of dirty old cloth.

"The rabbit tore up your doll to make her bed warm for her babies," Papa said. "They like to do that." I looked at Papa sadly. "Oh, well, the doll was too dirty to play with anyhow," he told me and I knew Nannie had been right. Grownups did study dirt, and close their eyes to the softness and love it sometimes covers.

Nannie and I left the smokehouse and sat in the arch of the big oak tree in my front yard, just right for two little girls to sit in and talk over their problems.

Nannie spoke to me in her soft voice, "Maybe the All-Seeing Eye's like grownups. Maybe it don't pay to bother him with things grownups don't understand. Maybe . . . ." Her voice trailed off into deep thoughts, and we sat quietly awhile until she spoke again.

"You can have my baby." She gave a little chuckle. "She's so dark to start, dirt don't show on her so bad."

I shook my head, careful not to let Nannie see the longing in my eyes.

"I have the baby rabbits, Nannie. I'll give you one."

"They get plum cute when they grow some," Nannie assured me. "They let you hold them, and they feel good hiding in your neck. We just made like our babies was alive, but now we'll have something that is."

Nannie stopped talking and pointed to the four-windowed cupola of Mr. Grumbley's barn. Her voice dropped to a whisper. "Maybe I was a little wrong about the All-Seeing Eye not bothering with our troubles. Maybe he don't see our way every time, but sometimes our way ain't too clear. Look around you. How far can you see?"

I couldn't see too far, I had to admit, with the trees and the rolling hills stopping my sight on every side.

"Could we climb into the cupola, Willard, we maybe could look ahead and see as far as the All-Seeing Eye," Nannie said.

I nodded, and imagined the softness of a real live bunny baby nestling close to my neck.

When I was seven, they told me we were moving to another town. The parsonage would be larger than the one we had. It would have an upstairs. A cement walk ran all the way to town. There would not be a clay lane.

When I told Nannie, she turned her back quickly, holding her head very high. "Who you think is goin' to keep care of you now?" Her voice was so still and low. I could scarcely understand what she said.

I hadn't thought of life without Nannie. I looked out at the pastures where we had picked daisies and run, hand in hand, against the wind. We cried, then, in each other's arms. It was the only time I ever saw Nannie in tears.

And that wasn't for long. Right away she choked and wiped her eyes on the backs of her hands. "I do believe we're forgetting something," she said solemnly. "Same wind blows where you goin' as blows here, ain't it? Same angels in same clouds!" Her eyes took on a mystical light.

"Folks has to grow up to hear—and see—something. But we're growin' fast, ain't we?"

She looked me up and down. "Maybe the wind will tell me what you're thinkin' and doin', times when I want you real bad."

When I didn't stop crying, she patted my shoulder. "And after you learn to set still and listen, I reckon the wind will tell you about me."

I was a little comforted then. For Nannie had promised that I, too, would grow up.

A Cobblestone Road Between

WE moved our furniture by wagon the short distance from the Todd County Circuit to Russellville. Papa hired a two-horse surrey with a fringed top for the family. Russellville, being an aristocratic town which boasted two colleges, would not welcome the new Methodist minister's family seated on a wagon.

As we entered the long rectangle that formed Main Street, we saw that wear and tear from mule and horse hooves had transformed the limestone rocks used for paving into smooth oval shapes, like giant eggs squeezed side by side. (Many a stone bruise appeared on a naked heel when a small foot slipped into the crevices.) Rubber-tired buggies with good springs jarred their passengers less roughly on this road than the steel-rimmed wagons and cheaper buggies less wealthy people used.

As we drove up to it, I looked at the big parsonage in awe. An iron fence, fancy with its wrought iron posts, was in front of the house. A short walk from the gate led to the small porch, four steps up from the ground. There was even a concrete walk leading to town. The house was a big gingerbread type with fancy gables. It had a large entrance hall, parlor, living room, dining room, kitchen, and servants' room at the end of the long back porch. Upstairs were four bedrooms, and I quickly claimed the small front one over the entrance hall that faced the street. My sisters, glad to be rid of me from their crowded rooms, I'm sure, aided me in my request.

The parsonage, built to accommodate the size of the families of ministers of that day, stood in the same yard as the church, and Papa had only to walk across the backyard to reach his office in the basement of the church. I think Mama was a little relieved to have Papa out of the house with his lapboard, scattered books, and writing equipment. It was hard to clean around his litter, though no one ever dared to call it that, especially when he was making charts about the prophecies on long rolls of unbleached domestic. Papa let me help him print the words when I learned to spell well enough, which was a real incentive for learning. Now all this equipment could go to the office in the church.

It did for awhile, but Papa soon brought his lapboard back to the sitting room where it was placed across the arms of his favorite rocking chair. Little by little he began to write his sermons in a place where he could read a sentence or two to Mama for her approval. Mama had an uncanny way of answering "yes" and "no" at the proper times, for I am sure she didn't listen with the concentration Papa expected. I saw her lips moving sometimes as she whispered her favorite song. "His grace is enough for me, for me," and as I grew older, I realized that it had become her theme, for as a minister's (especially Papa's) wife, she needed it.

The Browder house, its red brick with white trim imposing to a country child, was across the street. It had no front yard, but its alcoved door was directly on the sidewalk. A porch jutted from each side, and the yard was beautifully tended. It was the only yard I'd ever seen that had a gardener, and I was impressed, even though he also served as houseboy. To make the Browder household even more impressive there was Zone, the cook. We had no servants at our house, for Papa said that no matter how much money there might be, he wanted his girls to learn how to keep house. Sometimes, seeing the sloppy way some of my sisters did their chores, I wondered if Mama agreed.

Later on, when I knew them better, there were times I envied the Browders their fine way of living and the beautiful house, but I'd comfort myself with the thought that their house didn't have a beautiful church in its yard with a tall steeple reaching for the sky. And there were no clumps of wire grass in their manicured lawn to braid into pigtails so you could make believe you had a little girl of your own.

Mrs. Browder sat on the side porch mornings and late afternoons in the summer. She was dressed in black, unrelieved by a touch of color except for the jewels that glittered on her tiny white hands. Her hair was pure black, in direct contrast to her husband's white hair. Mr. Browder had a white mustache, too. Twice a day he walked to his office in town to practice law, his gold-headed cane tapping on the pavement to go with his twinkling blue eyes and smile. When he spit, it was never on the sidewalk, as others sometimes did, but in the grass or a bush. He wiped his lips carefully and unless you saw the spit itself you'd never know he chewed tobacco. Mr. Browder was a gentleman.

The first afternoon we were there, I sat on the curbstone in front of our house, my bare feet in the gutter that bordered the road, looking across the street at the beautiful child who sat on the porch reading. I wished that magic would transform her into Nannie, for no one could ever take Nannie's place.

"Why don't you come over?" the child asked. I wished for Nannie's hand to give me courage to approach this blue-eyed, golden-haired, fairy child. I ran a hand through my short, straight red hair and looked down at my stubby feet.

"Oh, come on over," the voice was impatient now, and not to be denied. I ran across the street and sat on the marble steps, drinking in the girl's beauty.

"You must be the new preacher's daughter." It was a statement. "My name is Harriet, and I live here with my grandmother."

My mouth fell open with astonishment. Grandmothers were to visit, not live with. Mothers were for that.

Harriet held up the book she was reading. "Do you like to read?"

I hung my head. I hadn't learned to read. It was more fun to play house in the tree roots and run in the wind with Nannie instead of studying. I felt Harriet's eyes on my bare feet and wished that I'd dressed for the afternoon as Mama had advised. An older girl (Betsy, who, I learned, was a visiting cousin), dressed like Harriet in shiny pumps and starched dress, came to the door. She eyed me critically, probably thinking I was some stray waif, then said curtly, "Go home!"

"Yes, do go home!" Harriet echoed. Mortified, I ran. The cobblestones felt as hot to my feet as the tears that stung my eyes. I ran upstairs to the little room that Mama had said was mine and lay across the bed, looking at the towering brick house across from ours.

Its long narrow shutters were partly closed, and I shivered, longing for the tiny house we'd left in the country that held so much fun and laughter.

The only time I ever saw Mrs. Browder leave her home was the next afternoon when I answered a knock at the door and she stood there with Harriet.

"Come in," I said, almost overcome.

I led them into the parlor, which had been hastily straightened for early visitors, and called Mama. We sat on the stiff mohair chairs which were furnished by the parsonage committee and which scratched bare legs unmercifully. They were very substantial—maybe because no child in his right mind would sit on them.

"I'm sorry if Harriet was rude to you yesterday...." She paused, waiting for my name.

"Willard," I hated to acknowledge that it was my name; it belonged to a boy.

"Willard," the way Mrs. Browder said my name it sounded like something special.

The next day I was enrolled in the Primary Department of Logan Female College. Harriet was not at school. That afternoon as we played in her yard, she explained about the educational system in Russellville.

"Real poor children go to the public school, middle class ones to yours. And—" She paused, trying to think of the best way to say, *high class*— "I go to Miss Bowden's Private School."

There was a girl in my room whom I much admired for her spells of fainting. I loved the way she cried, too, wiping her tears on real kid gloves which she kept daintily in one hand. (None of the rest of us had kid gloves; we were lucky even to have woolen mittens.) The attention she always got when she fainted filled me with a deep envy. My seven-year-old mind decided that if I could do the same, I'd be the center of attraction, too.

We sat on a long bench for recitations, and I chose the seat nearest the hot round stove, hoping its heat would aid me in my act. I did get too warm, and felt a little sick. I rolled my eyes (dramatically, I hoped) and moaned, letting myself slip off my seat gently onto the floor.

Our teacher quickly asked two of the big girls to lead me home, and I made, between them, a most satisfying exit. Eyes rolling all the way home, and suffering at proper intervals, I let the girls lead me to Mama at the kitchen door. She put her arm around me and thanked the girls. She led me to the empty living room couch and eased me down.

"I know the best remedy for fainting there is," Mama said kindly—very, very, kindly. Exultation filled me. My act had gone over. Maybe Mama would bring me a cool lemonade, a treat beyond comparing. When I heard her footsteps I peeped to see the size of my drink. Papa's half pint aluminum cup, no less!

Eyes closed carefully, I felt Mama's arm under my shoulders, raising my head.

"Drink all of it, honey, it's the best thing I know for fainting spells."

I took a taste and shuddered. Epsom salts, enough to taint the lukewarm water the cup contained. I looked at Mama. Were her eyes twinkling a little?

"Drink it all," Mama's voice was firm now, and I knew that the cup must be drained to the bottom, for the bitter drink was the only way I could save my face.

When I was through, Mama took the cup and said, "A day in bed will make you like new."

I started to take a book from the shelf, but Mama said quietly, "No reading, just quiet and rest."

At times I've been sick or badly hurt enough to do it again—but from that day to this I have *never* fainted!

I went with Harriet to eat her lunch when she came home from school in the afternoon. It awed me to walk down the wide hall toward the huge dining room. Heavy, red velvet draperies covered alcoves on each side of the front door with its semicircle of stained glass overhead.

The dining room was very large, and had a massive sideboard topped with a shiny silver service. The table was larger than ours, which seated all ten of our family, and I wondered why three people needed such a big one. It must be hard to pass food from such distance. (The riddle was solved the first time I ate with them, for Zone, dressed in fresh apron and cap, came from the kitchen to serve us. No one seemed to have much appetite, and I felt greedy as I took a huge slice of meat from the platter, remembering the one small portion we were allowed at our table.)

Harriet walked to a small window between the dining room and kitchen where her lunch stood on a tray. I couldn't imagine so many dishes of food at the same time. Harriet ate a little out of two of the dishes, then pushed the tray away in disgust.

"I don't see why Zone cooks the same things all the time."

I tried to make my voice as casual as I could with my mouth watering as it was. "Why don't you ask your grandmother to have her fix something else?"

"Grandmother is a woman of sorrow. She can't be bothered with little things."

"A woman of sorrow?" I didn't understand.

"One of my uncles died five years ago." Harriet spoke as if that were explanation enough.

"Let me help you put the dishes away." I wanted to get into the big kitchen.

"I don't have any duties except picking up my clothes." I thought of the big stack of silver I had to dry every night and the slop jars I had to empty and clean every morning, and other chores. It must be nice to be a lady.

At supper that night I took my sausage out of the dish and tried to capture two crumbs that were floating in the gravy. Mama took the dish out of my hands.

"No fair taking more than your share." I looked at her hands, big and rough and alive. I thought of Madam Browder's hands which reminded me of the dead white kitten Nannie and I had found on a coal pile. As Mama's warm hand brushed mine I wondered if Madam's hands felt as cold as the kitten when I stooped to touch him, and I was glad Mama wasn't a woman of sorrow.

Harriet was good at thinking up new games and was nice about letting me be first. I was first the time we played the jumping game. I remember how the bottoms of my feet stung when I got up enough courage to leap from the high lattice fence that separated the Browders' front lawn from their garden. I waited for Harriet to jump, but she climbed down.

"The game is getting dull, let's play something else," she said.

The day Harriet broke her finger we were playing in our yard. Papa took her on his lap, waiting for Mother to call the doctor. He pressed her head against his shoulder expecting her to cry, I suppose. She looked awkward sitting there, straight and white, like she hadn't sat on anybody's lap before. She looked at me hard, as a sympathetic tear rolled down my cheek.

"Grandmother says no lady ever cries in public." She was trembling now, and I wished I knew how to tell her the way tears washed the trembling away.

Spring came, and with it my first dress to be made from a piece of new material, cut from a whole bolt of gingham. My sister Nell had been teaching in the public schools that year; I couldn't believe my good fortune when she told me to go with her to town after school to pick it out.

It was so hard to decide between all the beautiful colors and patterns. I favored one with a bright red background dotted with white, but Nell talked me out of that.

"Red just doesn't go with your hair," she decided, so we bought a deep blue with white flowers.

"Please don't wrap it up," I begged the saleslady. "I want to show it to everyone on the way home."

Which I did, stopping at each door on the street, ringing the front doorbell, and displaying my treasure to the one who answered the bell.

"My dress won't be made out of my sisters' old clothes," I bragged. "See, it's all one piece."

When I went to share my surprise with Harriet, she was opening a box of underwear. For a moment I forgot my prize, marveling at the sheer beauty of the hand-embroidered garments with whipped-on lace. My breath came out all at once. Harriet opened a dresser and dumped the whole pile inside, still folded.

"Mother has them specially made for me every year by some nuns in Paris," she said indifferently.

My underdrawers were almost always made from

flour sacks, but I held my dress out defiantly. "My mother will make my dress."

Harriet touched the material. There was a disdainful note in her voice. "My mother doesn't sew; she's a lady." Suddenly her hand reached out and slapped my cheek hard. Her voice trembled.

"Go home!"

I clutched my dress fabric, not understanding. Tears splotched it as I ran home across the cobblestone road.

I sobbed my story out to Mama when I got home, and instead of comforting me, all she said was, "Poor little girl!"

Poor little girl, nothing! I sniffed to myself. Why did Mama pity *her*?

The next week the flu epidemic started. Madam Browder was ill with a nurse, and Zone left to care for some of her own people. To help out, Mother had Harriet eat at our table. I envied her manners that first meal, as she sat calmly wiping a bit of jam off on her napkin. Jam tasted good from a finger. I couldn't understand her lack of appetite.

A week later we sat at the supper table side by side. My sister Katherine had the flu and Mother looked tired. Her hair was stringing out of the big pins and the comb she wore to hold it up in the back. Her dress wasn't too fresh. I saw Harriet watching her, but I couldn't read her thoughts.

Mother spooned out onto each of our plates a generous serving of the jam she saved for the Presiding Elder's visit. It gave me an adventurous feeling to be eating it without his austere presence at the table.

I reached for the last biscuit on the plate, but Harriet's hand got it first. Her jam was gone, I saw.

"Trade you half my jam for half your biscuit." Then I blushed, remembering Harriet's perfect manners.

She broke her biscuit in two and laid half on my plate. I spooned half my jam and put it on hers. We broke our bread into bits and sopped the jam's sweetness, but some of it was still left on our plates. Papa, seeing the jam that was left, smiled at us, broke his remaining biscuit in two, and held out a half to each of us. Harriet and I ran to him and he held us close for a minute. Harriet didn't seem to mind at all.

We went back to our seats and ate the rest of our jam, wiping our plates clean, then licking our fingers one by one.

Harriet had forgotten to be a lady, and I felt better about my own shortcomings.

15

Loaf Bread Time

IT was our second spring in Russellville. I lay on my cot, shivering with excitement, and wondered, as I had last Christmas Eve, if the night would ever pass. I whispered a laughing goodbye to my small room. Tomorrow Mama would start spring cleaning and for five nights it would be anybody's guess where I'd sleep. Tomorrow would usher in the big week that heralded six days of store-bought food and loaf bread every meal.

Mama didn't clean like most of the women I knew in our small southern town—taking a room at a time and closing it, when finished, against dirt stirred up by brooms and beaters. Instead, she would spend the week moving furniture inside the house and out, opening drawers that hadn't been used for anything but hiding places all year. Watching to see what the drawers offered was one of the nicest things about housecleaning Mama's way. That, and the sketchy meals Mama set out anywhere.

I slipped into sleep, anticipating the taste and smell of loaf bread, which I'd buy at the baker's six whole days for the family; not once would we have our usual fare of corn bread or hot biscuits. Eating was just a necessary evil during spring cleaning time—to be put behind as quickly as possible. And loaf bread, Mama said, was her salvation from the cook stove.

When morning finally came, I hurried to the store. On my way home, I reached inside the paper bag and pinched off a corner of one loaf of the bread, enjoying the smell as I lifted it slowly to my mouth.

When I got home, the hall was full of furniture, stacked at every angle. At once I became an Indian, and sneaked my way through the mountain pass that led to the kitchen. I stood in the door watching Papa, his pencil hanging at a precarious slant behind his ear, as he carried the dining room chairs outside. Papa didn't look like he did every day in his office in the basement of our church. His face wore a bewildered expression, as it had when something he didn't understand came up in his congregation. I watched until the last chair was carried into the yard, then I ran through the canyon in the long hall and out the front door.

I jumped off the high porch, secure in the knowledge that everyone was too busy to warn me not to hurt myself. I ran toward the big chair in the yard that usually stood near the fireplace in the living room, ready to bounce into it, just as Papa came around the corner of the house, holding a wire beater.

Papa looked at me, and I stopped to hear what he was saying. "I'll be glad when this orgy is over." He looked longingly at his office next door. His beater made thumping sounds on the chair, and spirals of dust from carpet sweepings rose and disappeared into the air.

Somewhere he had lost his pencil from behind his ear, and looked almost undressed without it. I laughed, and Papa grumbled, "I'm glad somebody can enjoy this ordeal."

One of my sisters came from the backyard, carrying a pan of lye soap suds and a stiff brush. She rubbed the bubbles over the chair, and the material looked too new to jump upon.

By the end of the day the house held an unfamiliar look. Not one of the ten rooms had anything familiar about it. I ran into the parlor, completely empty except for the mattress from Mama's and Papa's bed on the floor. My feet made a ringing sound as I ran to jump into the soft center. I lay on my back and tried to reach the ceiling with my toes. I thought it nicer than having to sit sedately on the scratchy, stiff-backed, horsehair chairs when company came.

I looked at the high, narrow windows, bare to the street, and thought how big they looked without the blinds and lace curtains that usually covered them. I stood on tiptoe to touch the outlines on the wallpaper left by pictures that had hung there. The parlor took

85

on an air of adventure. I ran to find the pictures, and it was like a game of hide-and-go-seek, looking for familiar things in unfamiliar places.

I found the pictures on the porch, upside down, and laughed when I saw our family group standing on its collective head, Papa still dignified in his preacher suit, Mama and the girls resplendent in stiff, starched, white shirtwaists, and myself in the front row, pouting as usual.

I went into the backyard where Mama was supervising the quilt washing. Lonie, the woman who made this her specialty, was standing before the big black wash pot, pushing down bulges the covers made on top of the boiling water. I liked the whooshing sound the air made escaping as she poked the ridges down with her long wooden paddle.

Part of the line was hung with blankets, feather beds, and bed ticks. Later in the week Papa and I would fill the clean ticks with the fresh bales of straw which someone from the country had put on the back porch.

We ate dinner in the living room, standing or sitting around like a picnic. Papa looked uncomfortable trying to adjust his long legs on a footstool. I took two slices of loaf bread and covered them generously with jelly. I liked jelly for my noon meal, instead of the vegetables Mama regularly served. I knew there were cookies, too, for Mama always baked a supply the Saturday before spring cleaning week.

I took my paper plateful of sweets to the porch and sat on a bale of hay, reveling in the chaos Mama had created in one morning. I wouldn't have to rest after dinner or dress for the afternoon. Maybe I'd sleep in the kitchen that night, as I had last year one glorious time, and open the pie safe again. It would be fun to eat from its dark treasures once more by the light of the midnight moon. But that night my cot was folded under several boxes, so I slept on a folded quilt beside Mama and Papa in the parlor.

During the week I thought of several things I'd like to do to help, but my sisters, who were much older than I, shooed me away. They said I was too little to wipe walls with the long-handled, rag-tied broom. Beating carpets on the line got tiresome after a few whacks, and there was no one to play with. Nobody would think of letting their children interfere when someone was spring cleaning, and my sisters were cross when I begged them to help me find clean clothes so I could go visiting.

By Wednesday I wanted to play paper dolls, but they were safely hidden in the bottom of my dresser, where I'd put them so that my time could be spent in a more interesting way. There wasn't even a path to that dresser.

Thursday Mama had to remind me three times to go to the baker's for bread. I looked at my soiled dress, and she said it didn't matter, since I was just a child, and nobody would notice.

Friday, when I walked into the parlor, I saw that the curtains, starched and stretched to their full capacity, hung at the windows. There was a fresh smell pervading the house. I made my way to my little room. It was stacked with furniture, and I closed the door quickly against the crowdedness that pushed me outside. Wearily, with nowhere to go, I sat outside in my swing. But something seemed to be wrong. I looked at my empty hands, then went to the kitchen safe to get the biscuit I always nibbled when I was swinging. I opened the door and saw a loaf of baker's bread, left from the day before. I didn't want it, even covered with jelly. There were no biscuits.

That night I slept on my cot, just outside my door, reaching my hand to touch my wallpaper with its raised design. I went to sleep, thankful that darkness covered the outlines of the furniture usurping my place.

Saturday night Mama lined us up in the kitchen for our baths. Everything was in its place, and the cleanliness warned us to watch our steps. Once again the house, to eyes used to the helter-skelter of the past week, took on an alien air.

Before I climbed the stairs to my room to savor the smell of my fresh straw tick, I stopped in the parlor. I went to the window and watched the light from the street corner lamp shining through the clean glass.

It was then that I got the scent from the lace curtain, a hint of dust that no amount of washing and starching could quite replace. Forgetting my awe of the clean house, I buried my face in its folds, and the curtain was a promise that tomorrow would end loaf bread time.

I wondered if Papa's text next day would be the same as last year after spring cleaning. Something about washing the outside of a cup while the inside stayed dirty. I remembered how earnest he'd been, that day, and the genteel nudge one of my sisters had given Mama.

When Monday came, Mama would serve us corn bread at noon, piping hot, and if I ever again asked for jelly at dinner, Mama would shake her head, telling me that eight-year-olds didn't need too many sweets.

I looked at the parlor carpet, with its mingled

shadows, and saw again my paper dolls scattered across the floor on mornings when the older members of my family didn't need the room. Gaily I laughed.

Spring cleaning was over at last. And somehow I knew that a week of loaf bread time was enough for Mama, too.

16

The Cherry Girls

IT was in Russellville that I began to recognize my older sisters as individual personalities. My oldest sister, Mary, had been my mother figure since Mobile left, and it was in her that I put my complete trust. She was always gentle. David had sharp insight, and expected more of me than I thought myself able to do. Nell was a kind of special sister. Although she was ten years my senior, we shared in many things she couldn't or wouldn't share with her sisters who were nearer her own age.

It was to me that she read the poetry she composed lying along the wide branch of the sycamore tree. She let me roam the fields with her on her search for inspiration.

She talked *with* me, not *to* me, something that most older folks never did.

Sometimes we would go into Papa's office and examine his sermons. They were always written in pencil, and Papa preferred the carpenter's wide-lead variety. We often told him his writing looked like it was done with a stick of stovewood. He used lined tablet paper.

One day while Papa was safely away visiting, Nell and I were reading the sermon for the next Sunday. Nell, as usual, was several pages ahead of me. She began to laugh. I ran to see what amused her.

Nell was reading the marginal note, where the arrow from Papa's pencil pointed. "Cry here," was printed in block letters. Together we read the page to see the reason for tears. It was a story of harrowing grief. Death, suffering, and retribution stalked every page. Papa's dramatic gene was plainly showing.

On Sunday when the sermon was delivered, there were no dry eyes at this point—well, only four dry eyes. Nell and I managed to cover our uncontrollable laughter very nicely behind the security of handkerchiefs, which were always used by ladies when weeping.

Elizabeth, who was organized and efficient, sometimes scared me with threats which she carried out behind my parents' backs. But Katherine was always the same. I shared dishwashing with her, and to make the time pass she helped me name the silverware as I dried it. The ugly pieces were called by the names of those church members we didn't like, and the spoons, especially, corresponded to their characteristics. The most crooked one, which had to be constantly rubbed with sand and wood ashes to keep it usable, we named Mr. Storm, after one of the stewards in Papa's congregation. I got a lot of pleasure rubbing gritty sand into the spoon bowl, imagining it to be his face. He watched every move I made in church (I believed) and reported on my wayward ways. Mama had collected six silver tablespoons, which we didn't use every day. When I got to dry them on Sundays and special occasions, I did it with pleasure, laying each one carefully in a drawer and calling each by its name, for they honored some nice people whom I loved.

The older girls, except Mary, went to Logan Female College when we first moved to Russellville, and Mama and Papa considered the school a real blessing. Mary started teaching that year at the country school in Allensville, where she met Robert Coleman. The day they were married was a sorrowful one for me. As she appeared at the top of the big staircase in her white wedding gown and started down the steps where the groom waited for her, I began to sob aloud. My sisters tried to "shush" me, using pokes from an elbow or an unobtrusive pinch, but all I could see was the empty place in our house Sister would leave. I hated Robert and refused to tell him goodbye when they left. He had stolen my most valuable possession. My sisters, except Katherine, were humiliated, and scolded me severely afterward. Katherine took me into the backyard and helped me make a farm with stick fences, then slept with me that night.

Just before Mary left, Papa took all of us to the photographer's in town and had a family picture made, much against my will. I had enough of the family every Sunday as Papa made us line up outside the church door and we marched two by two down the aisle to our seats next to the front pew. The picture showed the rest of the family in their stiff starched shirtwaists and serge skirts, Papa in his best clothes, all smiling pleasantly. They put me in the front, and the photographer made me place my hands in my lap (I always hated my hands and was sitting on them). I tried to work them into the smallest knot I could, and sat there scowling fiercely.

David started teaching away from home the second year we were in Russellville. She may have felt sorry for me and a little guilty about her scolding at Mary's wedding, for she invited me to spend a week with her in the country school. It was my first time away from home, and I soon knew the meaning of homesickness. The parsonage looked good to me on Friday afternoon when we returned.

While I was gone, I discovered that Papa had bought a big dictionary—it was *Webster's Unabridged*, and stood on a metal stand. (Katherine and I had to wear our last year's coats that winter. Mama often said that if we could eat books we'd be better fed.) Papa may have bought the dictionary in self-defense. The older girls, conscious of the higher education of the Russellville parishioners, watched every word Papa used in the pulpit, waiting to pounce like a cat at a mouse hole on any mistake he made. Papa had a reputation to uphold in a far different kind of church from the ones to which we were accustomed. There were many differences in the people, but I could never understand the family's criticism.

Nothing pleased Papa more than to take his family walking on Sunday afternoon. Sometimes we would stop by one of the church member's front yards and sit outside with the family and visit. Highlights came when we were served ice cream and cake as an extra treat. One family we visited consisted of two older women and their brother who wore dresses and drooled all the time. He was past fifty and his sisters kept him entertained by tying long strings in yards of knots and letting him untie them. At first, waves of nausea hit me when I looked at him, but after I started to save string for him I looked forward to these visits. This was Katherine's suggestion. She helped me tie the knots and helped turn my loathing for the man into a desire to help him. His sisters used a lot of rags caring for him and Mama let me take them one of my worn-out dresses one day. It was a fulfilling moment for me.

Papa liked to introduce his daughters to someone new. He'd start with, "This is Mary, my Madonna. This is David, the beautiful one. This is Nell, the brainiest one. This is Elizabeth, the one who can paint. This is Katherine, the best-tempered one." He'd pause then, scratch his head, and end with, "This is Willard, the youngest one." One day, longing for a nice adjective to go along with my name, I asked Mama, "Am I pretty?"

Mama smiled, and said, "Yes, you are pretty in two ways." I began to feel good, but when Mama finished, "Pretty ugly and pretty apt to stay that way," my feathers fell. Children didn't get too many compliments in that day, expecially when they asked for them.

The Mob

RUSSELLVILLE was full of tension that year. A group of men calling themselves "the Nightriders" was determined to raise the price of tobacco, Logan County's leading crop and best source of income to the farmers. The leaders refused to sell tobacco at the low price offered, and when some farmer, needing money for his family or operation of the farm, sold his small supply, the Nightriders retaliated by scraping his next hotbed where his plants were started or, if tobacco had matured to the drying stage in the barn, by burning it down. Meetings were held on the public square in the middle of the night. The Nightriders attended in their white draped outfits. The horses were also covered in white sheets.

I longed to slip out and hear what was said. I suspected that Nell, my most daring sister did, and when I wondered aloud to her one day who was hiding behind the white masks, she said, "You'd be surprised if you knew." One day, while visiting one of my friends in the country, we were playing in the barn. We climbed the logs to the loft, a favorite pastime of all of us adventurous ones, and I saw in one corner, partly covered with the hay, something white. Before I could investigate, the girl's father came into the barn, and in a voice I'd never heard him use before, ordered us down. I supposed that he was afraid we'd be hurt, or I tried to think that, for he had been one of my favorite people, often taking me in his buggy when he passed by going to town. He just couldn't be one of those dreadful figures who paraded at midnight down the street! But the next time he passed by in his buggy and offered me a ride to town, I pretended I was busy and couldn't go.

Papa was upset over the burning of barns and scraping of plantbeds, and said so from the pulpit, taking to task those who did such dastardly acts. He remained calm—for him—until the Nightriders began tarring and feathering men or beating them unmercifully. The first time he heard of this his wrath could not be contained. From the rostrum he called upon law and order to take over, and urged all true and honest citizens to demand a stop to such atrocities.

Invitations to Sunday dinners, which had been numerous before, became rare from the country members, and church attendance dropped considerably. In spite of this, Papa continued to preach against the Nightriders, though I heard Mama once remind him of several places he'd had to move from after one year because of his stand on liquor or some controversial question. It took Mama a year after a move, she often said, to collect her wits, not to mention the expense. And a move meant upsetting the children after only a month in school, since the conference moved all ministers in October.

All of Papa's preaching didn't stop the Nightriders. Every time I was awakened from sleep by the clopping of hoofs on the cobblestone road, I trembled for fear that they would stop at our house and demand that Papa come outside and go with them for some dreadful reprisal. Each time I heard the horses pass the parsonage, I was thankful that it was some other man who was about to get thrashed or tarred and feathered instead of Papa.

Each Sunday just before church, it seemed to me that the air was full of tension, especially if there had been some outstanding act of violence the week before, for the older ones knew that Papa would never withhold the way he felt.

"Danger be hanged," he said. "I have my immortal soul to consider." It was awe-inspiring to hear his ringing tones as he said this, but coward that I was, I wanted to see his body considered, too.

The phone rang one Sunday a few hours before church. Papa was asked to come to another church for a special service, and hurriedly he asked a retired minister who lived nearby to preach for him that day. Our family always sat in the second pew from the front, and as I scrambled for my usual seat on the outside of the pew, I noticed a poorly dressed man enter the church and sit in the front seat directly before me. Our Russellville congregation always dressed well, and I thought that his work clothes looked out of place. The man seemed very restless and I wondered how he came to be there.

It was the habit for the congregation to rise as the minister entered from the side door, but the man remained seated, and I saw his hand reach into a side pocket of his coat. His eyes were fixed on the door. Only when he saw the retired minister enter instead of Papa did the man's hand relax, and he removed it from his pocket. I thought his shoulders sagged like he was disappointed but when I relayed what I'd seen to the family at dinner they pooh-poohed it and told me not to let my wild imagination run away.

"But did you see how fast he left when church was over? He almost ran out!" I argued.

The older ones looked at each other, the look that always left me out, since I was so much younger. Anyhow, they thought it did, and I wasn't about to disillusion them. I learned a lot through those looks.

From then on, the old retired minister was one of my favorite people, for I was sure that without knowing it, he had saved Papa from being shot.

Several of the farmers who had been whipped were Negroes, and when the incident of the German peddler and his daughter occurred, it was the last straw.

The peddler camped in his wagon at the edge of town, as peddlers were allowed to do. During the night, four men came to the wagon, tied up the man, and raped his daughter. When the word went out, leaders in the town demanded that the peddler point out the men who had done this. Two white men and two Negroes were arrested and put into jail. The next morning, a friend of ours who lived on the outskirts of town got up at his regular time and started to the pasture to bring in the cow for milking. Day was just beginning, and as he walked toward the field he saw some objects swaying from a tall oak tree.

"I blinked my eyes," he told Papa. "I just couldn't believe what I saw. When I got closer, there were four men hanging from the tree. Someone took them out of the jail and hanged them." The friend was still white and shaken from the experience.

Anyhow, I thought, there was no report that the Nightriders had done this. There had been no procession past the parsonage that night, I knew, for however hard I tried to ignore them, and sleep through it all, I couldn't, ever. But I wondered if anyone I knew had been among the mob. After finding that sheet in the barn loft I was never again sure about people. Just knowing and liking them didn't mean they were immune to evildoing. And not everybody covered acts of violence with white robes; some of the worst deeds were committed by plain people in everyday clothes. Such thoughts filled the very air of the whole town with an uneasiness, and instead of the usual cheerful greetings there were inquiring looks that seemed to say, "Are you one of *them?*"

About a week after the hanging our telephone rang in the middle of the night. There was nothing unusual about this, for Papa, like all ministers of that day, stood ready to go into any home where there was trouble, whatever form it make take. Perhaps, I thought, someone was about to pass the crisis in an illness, or maybe die, and the family felt better having someone there who was familiar with the Lord, someone who devoted his life to such a calling.

I heard Papa and Mama talking in their room, and was getting ready to resume my sleep when my sister Nell came to my bed. "Get up and dress," she ordered me.

"Is the house on fire?" I asked, trying to figure why I was to dress before leaving, for Papa had stressed to us the importance of getting out of a burning house at once.

"Maybe," she said shortly, pulling my dress over my head.

I could hear the rest of the family downstairs at the

front door. "Where are we going?" I asked, excited by this new experience.

"To the Browders. They have a brick house and we will be safer there."

Bit by bit I learned what the call had been about. A Negro mob had held up a train in Allensville and 300 armed Negroes were bringing the train to Russellville to pillage the town that had hung two of their race. They had promised that not a single girl or woman would escape their vengeance, and the call from the telephone operator, or "Central" as we called her in those days, was a warning to every man in Russellville. The men were to meet at the railroad station, fully armed, leaving some to patrol the streets.

When we got to the Browder house, Papa and Mr. Browder left us, being sure that we sat on the winding stairway which had no windows to aid a bullet's entrance. Harriet Browder and I sat together, alternately shivering with excitement and fear.

I looked at the faces near me in the dim light. "Where are Mrs. Browder and Nell?" I asked.

"Grandmother is in her room praying and talking to Uncle Lucien," Harriet told me.

"But Uncle Lucien is dead!" I stammered in surprise.

"She talks to him every night," Harriet said indifferently. Uncle Lucien had been dead for some time, but it never occurred to me now to doubt that Mrs. Browder and Uncle Lucien communicated with each other. Such affairs were beyond question when participated in by remarkable folks like the Browders. Later, telling Papa about it, I noticed that he looked disapproving and didn't have much to say.

Nell's whereabouts soon came to light when we heard the stern voice of Mr. Browder at the door telling her in no uncertain terms to stay inside. Later, he said he had seen something creeping in the shadows and had called out, "Who goes there?"

"Me," replied Nell in a small voice.

"Then *me'd* better get back in the house and stay there!" I suspected that Mr. Browder rather admired her courage. She was always his favorite of the six Cherry girls. (I often wondered if it was his influence that caused Nell to give up the approved job of teaching, go to a secretarial school in New Jersey, and become a law stenographer. Later, during World War I, she went to Siberia with the Red Cross, an unheard-of thing for a girl to do in our community.)

I do not know how long we sat on the stairs, but it was still dark when we heard the men return.

"Somebody warned them that we were at the station armed," they told us, "so they made the engineer back all the way to Allensville."

"And I didn't have a thing on me except my pocket knife!" Papa was almost talking to himself. "Me, with six daughters!"

From that day not a man we knew was without at least some form of firearms. Papa invested in a huge, double-barreled shotgun, and kept it fully loaded by his bed, though only he was allowed to touch it.

Tension mounted fast after that, and the National Guard was brought in and camped on the outskirts of the town. One Sunday afternoon, Papa took me to visit the camp. I was greatly impressed by the uniforms and looks of determination, and I fell in love with one young soldier who gave me a smile.

Our playtime was limited from then on. We were

never allowed out of the sight of a grownup. The guards patrolled the sidewalks day and night. I never heard anything said about the use of any form of mediation. The guards were there to see that we were protected. They meant business, and there was no fear that later on they might be tried for some act of violence, as they might be today.

The Browders' yardman, fearing the atmosphere, I suppose, left for an extended visit to his folks who lived in another county. But Zone, the Browder cook, stayed on. She said little to us when we asked questions, refusing to get herself involved in any white folks' business, though it never occurred to me that she was any different from us. I just loved and accepted her as she was.

Little by little things began to ease up. The yardman returned and the guards left, much to my sorrow. The one who smiled at me came to church on Sundays and Papa's sermons fell on my deaf ears. The last day he attended church he stopped and said to me, "You remind me of my little sister." So *that* was why he'd smiled! Disillusioned to the point of illness, I went home by way of Papa's office. There the smell of old books, ink, and mold offered me their usual greeting. I sat in Papa's big leather chair, feeling very small and useless, left out completely from the adult world. There was no understanding grownups. I laid my head on the arm of the chair and must have gone to sleep, for I was awakened by Papa's voice calling, "Willard!" The door opened and when Papa saw me in the chair he came over and took me in his arms, holding me for a moment. He was trembling a little. I remembered the harsh realities of the days before, and knew that old people, too, had their problems. And they did love us, though it was sometimes shown in strange ways.

The next afternoon, feeling that all was well again, I slipped outside while the family was taking the afternoon rest and sat on the curb. I saw the grocery wagon approaching, pulled by a lanky mule. I often pulled grass for the mule and fed it while the driver went inside to deliver groceries. I ran into the street. The mule stopped, expecting more grass, and before the young black man could refuse, I climbed on the wagon seat with him. He started to say something, but I shook the reins and we were on our way. The trip was to the country, where one of Papa's parishioners lived, and it took quite a while to get there.

The cook came to the door to take the groceries, and gave me a hard look, then whispered to the driver. I couldn't hear, but when he came back he trotted the mule, saying nothing to me on the way. He pulled up in front of the parsonage, let me out, and drove on to town. I could hear the phone ringing and ran to answer it before one of the older ones could, for I feared that someone was tattling. I remembered Mama's answer when someone called to tell her of one of my misdeeds. "Thank you very much, but Willard has already told me about that." I said in my best voice, "Hello!" As soon as I hung up, I'd tell Mama myself.

"Oh, you got home all right." It was the voice of the cook to whom we'd delivered groceries.

"Sure," I said. There was a sigh of relief at the other end of the line, and I went to tell Mama all that had happened. After all, I'd proved that the nightmare was over, and that once again we could take our places as friends to our black neighbors.

18

Some Firsts

HARRIET and I were talking one afternoon as we sat on the curb that bordered the road between our houses.

"Did you know that there is going to be a moving picture show here next week?" she asked.

I shook my head, pondering how pictures could move and make a show.

"Grandfather is going to take you and me," she said.

I couldn't even answer, overcome with such good news. Then I thought about Papa and the way he felt about all worldly things. Harriet seemed to sense my dread of Papa's refusal, for she said, "Grandfather is going to ask your father." I sighed in relief. Papa respected Mr. Browder, and wouldn't be likely to refuse him this request. Earlier that summer he had let me go with Mr. Browder and Harriet to the Ringling Brothers Circus, and I could still remember the thrill of the three-ring performance—though I rather resented the fact that so much was going on at the same time, that, no matter how fast I moved my eyes, I still missed some of the most daredevil stunts.

Until the night for the show, I let my imagination run riot about moving pictures. I'd stand before a family portrait hanging on our wall, and wonder if the pictures shown would be moving from place to place in their frames.

I was trembling as we entered the small amusement hall where the picture was to be shown. I envied Harriet her coolness. Mr. Browder took my hand and led us down the dim aisle to our seats. On the stage there hung a big white sheet, and I supposed that the pictures would appear there. Suddenly the lights were put out, and from the back of the room came a point of light, and the noise of some kind of machine running. I screwed around in my seat to see what it was, and Harriet poked me in the side.

"Watch the screen, silly," she whispered. Lights and shadows began to glide across the screen, and suddenly they became pictures, jerky pictures of people and places, and the people moved in a very real way.

The story featured a madman, who slipped away from his nurse and led the ones who tried to recapture him on a long chase. I was especially impressed by the nurse in her uniform, white cap, and determined expression, and decided to choose nursing when time came for me to select a career. The music came from a piano, loud at the most terrifying points, soft in gentler scenes.

I couldn't say much on the way home, still living as I was with the brave nurse who ignored danger as she ran to the end of an ocean pier and held her patient until a uniformed policeman took him away. One young man lingered and held the nurse in a long embrace, which brought forth whistles and stomping of feet from the young bloods in the audience.

That same week I saw my first automobile. The

whole family ran to the front window when we heard an unearthly coughing and chugging in the street, and the scream of a frightened horse rearing in his buggy shafts, then bolting down the street in a runaway. The car was going fast, and in spite of Grandfather George Cherry's prediction at his fireside ("Ha! Imagine such a thing as a horseless carriage! It will never be! Ha!") there it was going down the street without a horse in sight. A man and woman sat in the single seat, much like a regular buggy's, the man holding some kind of stick with which he guided the thing. Blue clouds of smoke came from behind in constant puffs. The wheels were like buggy wheels, with tires of thicker rubber than usual horse-drawn vehicles. The lady was dressed in the same kind of long coat we wore when we drove on dusty roads in a buggy; her hat was covered with a veil and tied under her chin. She sat like a statue, perhaps amazed at the speed of the car, which we later heard made from fifteen to twenty miles an hour on a good level road.

People out for afternoon drives in their carriages trained their coachmen to get out at the first noise made by a car and hold the horses' heads until it passed and the danger was over. Papa preached a sermon or two against this intrusion on people's safety, but soon gave up the fight as other cars began to be seen on the streets. There was no way to stop "so-called progress," said Papa sadly, and people ignored the old adage, "Never buy anything you don't need lest you need something you can't buy."

"Who," he often said, "needed such newfangled, pretentious luxuries, when the Lord had provided them with horses and mules?"

When one of the men who drove a car suggested that mules and horses had taken the place of oxen, Papa looked thoughtful, scratched his head, and for once had no ready answer.

IT was about this same time that we had our first experience with a robbery.

We were sitting around the fire. I heard the melancholy wail of the train as it came into the station, and wondered, as usual, about the passengers.

A little while later, the front doorbell rang. Papa always went to the door at night. He returned with a middle-aged woman, shivering with the cold. She was shabbily dressed. We made room for her at the fire and she held out her red, chapped hands to the blaze.

It was the custom for the minister to care for any guest of his own denomination overnight, and many times we had done this. So, matter of factly, Mama went to the kitchen for a plate of food which the woman devoured hungrily. Mama fixed her a bed on the couch and we retired upstairs.

When we came down next morning, the couch in the living room showed signs of being slept on. Papa went to the kitchen to make the fire in the stove, but came back immediately.

"Did anybody unlock the back door?" he asked. We shook our heads.

"Where is she?" I asked.

As I walked through the dining room to the kitchen I noticed that the drawer that held our only silver spoons was open.

"They're gone!" I began to cry, and Mama came to me and felt through the drawer. "That's the noise I heard," I said. "In the night."

I noticed that Mama was not wearing her gold-rimmed glasses, and asked, "Did she take those, too?"

Mama nodded. Papa began to storm. "She's no Methodist! She's a liar, and any liar will steal! Imagine her saying *she* was a Methodist!" Papa was truly indignant at such an outrage, but I mourned the loss of our silver spoons.

"I was going to give her my mittens," Katherine said. "Her hands looked so cold."

"I hope they freeze plum off!" I was mad, and for once nobody reprimanded me or corrected my grammar.

19

Calhoun

I GUESS Russellville was the highest-class church Papa ever pastored. Sometimes he said the Louisville Conference was not fair to him sending him as it did to so many poorer congregations. The bishops reminded him that he was one of their preachers who had the ability to transform a less fortunate church into the best it could be. I overheard Mama say that she thought Russellville was a kind of bribe, to salve Papa's ego, to heal his wounds from being sent to so many less-prosperous places.

We went by train from Russellville to Livermore, ten miles up Green River from Calhoun. It was my first train ride, for the move from Elkton had been by carriage, followed by wagons loaded with our possessions. When we got on, I had held onto Papa's hand rather tightly, somewhat ashamed that such a big girl, all of ten, would be afraid of this monster with its loud whistle and enormous puffs.

Papa led us to our train seats, and let me have the one next to the window, which I immediately asked to be opened. I was sorry about this when a cinder from the track hit me in the eye, and whirls of smoke enveloped us as the train got under way. The seats were red plush, scratchy as burrs to my bottom, clad though it was in three layers of clothes. For awhile, after Mama got the cinder out of my eye and Papa had put the window down, I enjoyed moving the seat back and forth from erect to reclining position. I couldn't believe the speed we were going. Telephone poles and trees fled by, and small houses near the track with people on the porches seemed to vanish almost before they were seen. Most of the people waved and I waved back, feeling very sorry for those children doomed to sit on a mere porch while I flew by at the speed of lightning.

Mama had packed our lunch, and we ate, shooing away the flies which inhabited the passenger car. A tiny baby across the aisle from me was fast asleep. The flies crawled across its face. The mother, tired and pale, occasionally brushed them off with her thin hand. I couldn't see for the life of me how anyone could stand a fly creeping across his face.

Until we moved to Russellville, most of the people we knew didn't have screens, but I remembered how Papa had made a fly trap, and how he nailed cheesecloth across the windows to keep most of them under control.

For the shooing, we darkened every opening but one, since the light attracted them. Each member of the family (visitors helped too, when we had them) took a towel and, starting from the back shooed the flies to the light. It was my job to open the outside door for the hordes of flies to escape. Looking at the baby, I decided that family probably didn't bother to shoo flies.

When we stopped in Central City, a man got on the train. (They called him "Butch.") Around his neck he had a strap which held a tray, filled with candy, popcorn, cakes, and fruit. I looked at the tray longingly, and then the man stopped by our seat.

"Candy, peanuts, popcorn, cakes, oranges, bananas. Only five cents!"

Papa reached into his pocket and pulled out a nickel.

"Which do you want?"

I reached for a banana, then thought how quickly one could disappear and took an orange instead, the treat we had mostly at Christmas. Oranges lasted longer, and the peels could be saved and gnawed on for a long time, a kind of lasting reminder of their goodness.

The train started with its usual jerk, which I later discovered set you squarely on your behind if you happened to be standing.

When we got off the train in Livermore we collected our baggage. Mama always had an extra bag or two, and we teased her, saying that she would carry a sack of greens or something into heaven. There just wasn't room in the suitcases or satchels for Mama's last minute additions. We walked down to the river, where the mail boat was docked. It would take us to

Calhoun, ten miles up the river. I was excited about the boat trip, for we had lived inland and my only encounters with water were wading in rain-filled ditches.

During the trip up the river, Papa walked about, as he always did, for he was a restless man, talking to the two young men who ran the boat. Small boats like the one we were on passed us, pushing huge barges filled with sand, coal, or other materials, and I asked Papa how such a small boat could propel such a large barge. The young man told me that they sometimes transported two barges at once. This gave Papa a chance to expound on *inertia*, which I didn't understand at all, but listened to carefully, knowing how it pleased Papa to teach.

I pondered how I might impressively use the word on some new acquaintance in the next town but discarded the idea when I remembered the man who tried to impress Papa with his large vocabulary.

"Brother Cherry, when I get my com-pinion asphyxiated, it's mighty hard for anybody to con-sequence it."

Papa wasn't above reminding us of this if we ever used a word incorrectly. So I gave up the idea of trying to floor anyone with *inertia*.

The boat turned into the landing at Calhoun, and as always we were eager to see the town where we would be at least a year. There was a steep road from the river to the town, and later we learned Calhoun had been built on higher ground because of the floods that hit the area some springs. On each side, at the top of the hill, were two large buildings, one brick and one frame. Each one was a hotel, though the brick one, crumbly with age, was used only for occasional visitors.

We walked up the plank walks on Main Street, where stores had been built on each side. Many of them had extended roofs over the streets. The big courthouse was most imposing. Side streets were used for residences, I noticed, as we walked to the parsonage. Following the directions of the man on the boat (who later married my sister, David Ella), we turned aside on a street and at the next corner saw the church. It wasn't on the Main street like the Baptist and Christian churches, but I noticed it was brick, and when Papa said, "Well, it isn't too bad," Mama answered with a sigh, "Wait until we see the parsonage."

This parsonage looked very small after the home we'd had in Russellville. It was a one-story four rooms with a hall, a narrow front porch, and a summer kitchen at the back, joined to the house by a covered plank walk.

When we opened the front door, Mama began to sniff. Her nose led her to the back bedroom. We'd heard that the minister who preceded us had lost his wife while there, and his small children had sometimes failed to follow the path to the outhouse at the rear of the garden. Mama took one look at the beds and had Papa move the mattresses into an open space in the garden, where she added kerosene and burned them.

"We'll sleep on straw ticks," she said, "until our featherbeds come."

Mama turned a straight chair upside down and examined it, then removed her clothes and placed them on it, motioning for me to do the same. We got into work clothes and Mama went to the kitchen where Papa, knowing Mama's ways, had started a fire and put water from the cistern on to heat.

The back bedroom had two wooden beds, a dresser and washstand—scratched and finger printed, a ragged rug, and tattered curtains, which were promptly removed and added to the fire in the garden.

There were a few nondescript chairs about the house which Papa later repaired. There was an iron bed in one of the front rooms and an old rocker or two.

The kitchen was long and narrow. A table stood at one end with a bench and four chairs. The step stove was cracked and warped. A shelf near the back door held a water bucket and dipper.

Mama's nose had a way of twitching, and her eyes batted very fast when she was upset. They were racing now.

"Not much like the nice things we had in Russellville," I said.

Papa was looking over the outside, and seemed to feel compensated for lack of house room by the big garden—overrun by weeds, but well-fenced. It had rich-looking dirt, which he was sifting between his fingers when I ran out to see the outside, carrying an armload of slats from the beds to be scalded. Papa was always challenged by a garden and felt deprived when there wasn't one. Even in Russellville, where there was only a small backyard, he had taken a posthole digger and cut through the foot of ashes which had covered the ground, and planted tomatoes below them—tomatoes which, he bragged, covered a dessert plate when cut across. In this large area he could let his talent for raising food go, and our table would benefit greatly from fresh vegetables.

We set about getting beds ready for the night and cleaning up the house. Mama watched carefully for signs of bedbugs, while I hoped I'd get to see one, thinking they must be something the way Mama dreaded them. They must be, I thought, at least as big as a pound of butter and their bite ferocious. Once a rat ran across the kitchen floor.

Nobody came to see us. I dreaded my first day at school, which turned out to be a nightmare. I felt able to handle my fourth-grade teacher, but every time I looked around, curious eyes were eating away more of my composure.

When recess time came I sat on the wooden front steps, trying to hide my hands which I always thought of as ugly. The entire student body gathered around me in a semicircle, staring, and an occasional whisper made my hands and feet grow too big to hide. My long braids of red hair felt like ropes pulling my self-esteem into the dirt of the school yard.

It was then I had my first personal encounter with a Baptist, though at the time I didn't know her denomination, which Papa put next to Catholics in his esteem. She was the first grade teacher and she came to me and sat down, hugging me close.

"Shame on all of you." She spoke to the children. Her voice was soft, but carried authority. "Staring like a bunch of rude children! Myna Lee, come here."

A small girl about my age detached herself from the semicircle and came up.

"I'm sorry, Aunt Myra," she said. She held out her hand and I took it, feeling safe in the knowledge that she and Miss Myra were kin. We were soon absorbed in a game of drop-the-handkerchief and I was allowed to be first. My popularity seemed to increase, for the handkerchief was dropped behind me several times, once by a good-looking boy named Harry, who later raced me home from school most afternoons, jeering at me all the way. He was my first beau, even after I found out that he, too, was a Baptist.

The Crisis

OUR three years in Russellville had been good and I was reluctant to leave. People in our church in Calhoun shunned us. Mama explained that they must be remembering the last family who had lived in the parsonage. Papa's salary was a very meager one, and our savings from the Russellville church was almost gone. I felt forsaken, and a raging blizzard with zero temperatures outside didn't help.

It seemed like the last straw when Papa came down one night with an attack of acute indigestion. Mama tried all the usual remedies she used when we were sick, then called Dr. Haynes. When he came and felt Papa's side where he had the pain, he looked serious.

"I'm afraid it's his appendix," he told Mama. "We can't take him to a hospital, he couldn't stand the trip in a wagon in this weather, and he'd have to lie down." The snow was blowing outside and the wind made fearful noises through the cracks in the windows and doors.

"Could he go by train?" Mama asked.

Dr. Haynes shook his head. "We'd have to take him by boat to Livermore and he'd freeze to death in the baggage car if we got him to the train. I guess it's up to us."

I thought of two funerals of people who had died of acute indigestion, and went out of the room so that Papa couldn't see my tears.

Papa's fever rose during the night and as I lay in the back room I could hear him begging Mama to go to the back door and run off the man who was trying to get in. In his delirium he thought the wind beating the snow against the door was someone trying to harm his family.

"If you don't go, I will," Papa shouted. Sick as he was, he was ready to protect his own.

Mama's quiet, "Hush, Papa, it's only the wind," reassured me, for Papa had never said things without meaning them, and I'd begun to wonder if we were in danger.

Mama often said that without Dr. Haynes, who was a Baptist, Papa would never have lived. He came several times a day, staying hours, studying the medicines in his black doctor's case, choosing, discarding, until he decided which one to use. (We never got a bill for his services.)

It seemed that cash money was scarce too. When Papa first got sick I overheard Papa and Mama talking, and confided in Dr. Haynes. The next night a man and his two sons braved the blizzard. They had come to lend Papa some money.

"Money on the signature of a very sick, maybe dying man," Papa said in amazement to Mama after they left.

Later, I discovered they were also Baptists.

Mama didn't sleep night or day, keeping compresses on Papa's side. She hardly noticed when I came down with chicken pox and mumps at the same time.

I can see that sickroom now. Mama had hung quilts over the windows to shut out the cold, but blasts from the raging storm puffed them out like balloons, and the wind shrieked its way through the cracks. The fire in the grate burned brightly, warming a small area near the hearth. Occasionally a puff of smoke came down the chimney as a blast of wind came from a certain direction.

Every time Dr. Haynes came through the front door, it took all his strength to close it, and the floor in the hall was misted with a layer of fresh snow.

I cannot remember how long the blizzard lasted, but I do remember how much the wind sounded like shrieking demons the night of Papa's crisis. To my childish ears those demons were threatening, "We're coming to take Papa away!"

The shaking of my body got worse. I was hurting from mumps and itching from drying chicken pox. I lay alone in the back room, ignored by Mama, whose whole attention was focused on Papa in his delirium.

Loneliness overpowered me; there was no one except me in the whole hostile world. I thought of all the sins I'd committed, and the winds carried dire warnings. If the demon spirits got into the house and took Papa away, I'd be left without my best friend and protector.

I do not know how long I could have stood my misery. The door opened between the rooms and Dr. Haynes came in. He sat on my bed and began to take my pulse. He stuck a thermometer in my mouth and shook his head when he read it. Then he opened his little black bag and took out a couple of pills. He put his arm around me and handed me a glass of water. I swallowed the pills as he sat on my bed, and I began to wonder if Papa could be mistaken about Baptists. After all, they had been the ones who had stood by us when our own congregation had turned us down.

Later on, I noticed that never again did Papa tell the story about the preacher who used his three fingers to emphasize the points, "Repent! Believe! And be baptized!" The finger for the last word was bent entirely back.

Papa pulled through, an unheard-of miracle in that day when an appendix had ruptured and peritonitis had set in. As spring approached he began to sit in a chair in the pulpit to preach, which cramped his style no end. He was determined to make a garden, and one of the parishioners who had a team of mules plowed the land and got it ready for planting. When he offered to plant it too, Papa refused. He was so weak that he had to sit on a stool, and when this, too, tired him too much, he laid flat on the ground, easing himself along between the rows. Papa could never have tolerated a welfare state. He believed in self-reliance.

Christmases Past

DAVID, my oldest sister at home, often compared her own childhood with mine. She assured me that life was much better for me than it had been for the rest of the girls.

They discovered early that preachers' children were set apart from the usual way of living other children enjoyed. More was expected from them, and the parishioners had a perfect right (some took it as a duty) to watch, correct, and report on any questionable behavior. This was particularly hard on the Cherry boys, who inherited a lot of their father's independence.

My sisters learned to accept their roles in life. Each time they moved they hoped to find things better, knowing that the length of their stay in a town depended almost as much on their own behavior as on the way Papa preached and did his pastoral duties.

When I complained because I hadn't received a certain doll for Christmas, David told me about their first year in Bradenburg. On Christmas Eve, they hung their stockings over the fireplace, then went to bed early, eagerly waiting for Christmas morning. David noticed Mama's uneasiness as it got later in the evening.

When the girls got up they found their stockings hanging limp. Mama began to fill them with anything she could find, a cake of soap, a brush, or a comb, trying to make a joke of it. The girls couldn't see anything funny at all. So far there had always been something, at least an apple and a stick of peppermint candy if nothing else. Then Mama had an inspiration. Every year, when the church had a Ladies' Aid Society, they pieced and quilted several covers for the preacher's family. Mama got the stack from the chair and laid the quilts on the bed. "You can pick out whichever one you want," she told them. "You see, you do have something for Christmas."

The joy of the season was saved that year as the girls began to choose the patterns and colors.

It was customary in those days of hardship for one of the church societies to furnish Santa for the preacher's family. That year, one of the missionary societies had promised to do it, but the lady who was in charge got a call to a funeral out of town and forgot all about it.

Another year, in another town, the treasurer of Papa's church got angry with Papa over politics. In that town only Democrats were even recognized, and when Papa made some statement about what a pity it was that some Republican candidate had been assassinated, the treasurer was furious. So he refused to pay Papa the salary due him in December.

Since they already were living from hand to mouth, Papa and Mama knew that there would be no Christmas that year. The man's daughter was David's seatmate at school, and she knew what nice things Santa would bring her friend. David said it made her sad to know the difference in the gifts they would receive, but it hurt most of all to know that the father of the girl she loved could be so mean.

On Christmas Eve, David was walking in town and the treasurer stopped her. He said curtly, "Take this ten dollar bill and give it to your father. Tell him not to spend any of it on foolishness for Christmas, either."

Little chance of that, David thought, when food was so low. Papa's salary was only sixty dollars a month, and that hadn't been paid. Tears were running down her cheeks as she handed the bill to Papa and delivered the message. Neither he nor Mama said anything, but David said Mama's nose started twitching, a sure sign that she was deeply disturbed. The donations that customarily came in for Christmas, sometimes a whole dollar's worth of sugar, a bushel of potatoes, a slab of bacon, a pound of butter, canned fruit or jelly would be missing, for no one dared to face the wrath of the treasurer.

David told of one special Christmas that stood out. Ithiel, the oldest boy, was dating Lillian, a beautiful girl who belonged to Papa's church. Lillian came to Mama before Christmas and told her not to worry about filling the stockings.

"I shall never forget that day," David told me. "Our stockings were bulging. There was a little doll in each one, a book, some hair ribbon, candy, fruit, and nuts. We felt so fulfilled, and the empty stockings of the past years were forgotten."

"In comparing the Christmases," David said, "I wonder how people can be so mean, and so good?"

She went to her bureau drawer, removed a piece of material, and handed it to me. "I'll make you a new Sunday dress," she promised.

I thought that sometimes the *same* person could be very mean, and at other times very good. Like David and me.

22

The First Swim

THE second summer we lived in Calhoun an article by Annette Kellerman came out in the *Ladies' Home Journal*, explaining a simple way to learn to swim before entering the water. There was never a scarcity of magazines in our home. We did not always have shoes without holes in the soles or a new Sunday dress every year, but somehow the magazines continued to arrive every month. We devoured *Capper's Farmer*, *American*, *Liberty*, *Colliers*, *Saturday Evening Post*, *Christian Herald*, *Woman's Home Companion*, and others. Beginning with my twelfth Christmas I received *St. Nicholas* and the *Youth's Companion*.

Since I believed every written word, I read Miss Kellerman's article in absolute faith. She showed pictures of a would-be swimmer lying across a piano stool on her stomach, going through motions outlined in the illustrations. Coordination was the word, she said, and my stomach took on a permanent ring from the stool as I spent hour after hour learning to make my arms and legs do a perfect breast stroke in the air. Sometimes one of the family stood watching me with a quizzical look, but I ignored that person loftily, secure in the knowledge gained from Papa's reiteration, "The printed page doesn't lie. I know it's so; I read it in the newspaper."

When I was sure that my technique had been perfected, I began to urge Papa to take me to the river for my first swim. He suggested more practice for several days, but one day we started for the river. Papa carried a rope over his arm. That was a triumphant march. I told everyone I saw on the way that I was going for a swim. Everyone laughed.

We came to the water's edge and Papa tied the rope loosely around my neck. He stepped into a flat-bottomed boat and motioned for me to wade out into the water. The Green River looked deep and wide, and doubts began to take the place of my original confidence.

"Come on out deeper," Papa suggested.

Led by the gentle tug of the rope, I waded into the water.

"Come on, now, let's see you swim!" Papa said encouragingly. "Now!"

With a mighty effort, I thrust my arms before me in the position I'd learned on the piano stool, still standing on solid bottom.

"You can't swim standing up," Papa was chuckling now, and, determined I'd show him, I struck out, lifting my feet from the bottom. I made one try until, panic-stricken, I felt myself going down. It was a long way to the bottom. With the help of Papa's rope, my head reached the surface, and spitting water, I yelled, "Pull me out, pull me out!"

How Papa ever accomplished it, shaking with laughter as he was, is a miracle. Crestfallen, I waded to shore.

I was humiliated beyond belief. We started for home, Papa still shaking with laughter. When he started back by way of Main Street the way we had come, I ran to the back path across the field. How could I face the people to whom I'd bragged about knowing how to swim? Halfway home Papa called to me. "Willard, don't feel too bad. I'll teach you how to swim."

"You will?" I asked. "When?"

"As soon as your mammy gets you a bathing suit," Papa promised.

So, by way of explanations, I said that Mama was having suits made for all of us.

From the same issue of *Ladies' Home Journal* we ordered patterns for our bathing suits. My older sisters took part of their salaries from teaching to purchase the material, which consisted of a loosely woven dark blue serge that shed water instead of absorbing it. The full bloomers came down past the knees, and the middy blouses had full sailor collars extending halfway down the back. We wore black stockings which came under the bloomers, under-drawers, and camisoles. The more fully developed girls also added corsets and bras.

One by one the other girls in town joined us at our swimming beach with Papa doing the instructing. Before the summer was over he had us all doing creditable breast strokes, an exercise guaranteed to develop perfect womanly contours, according to Annette Kellerman.

By the second summer all of us (except Mama, who was afraid of the water, and who sat in it just past her waistline, bragging, "Look how far I'm out!") learned to swim. It was a proud day when Papa and I swam across Green River and back without touching shore.

Swimming was a neighborhood affair. Many afternoons we took our skillets with us to the shore and cooked our suppers. We used whatever we had: corn, potatoes, bacon, fish, chicken, or eggs. These events were times when denominations were forgotten. "Campbellites" (a name Papa chose to give the sect which preferred to call themselves "Christians," explaining that no one denomination had a right to that title) and Baptists joined us at the river bank.

Once when we were swimming in Green River, Papa stepped on a broken whiskey bottle and almost cut off his big toe. He came out of the water bleeding, holding the culprit bottle shard in one hand. He glared at the piece of sharp glass malevolently.

"Whiskey, the devil's tool," he pronounced, while we who were swimming with him looked on, dismayed at the free flowing blood. Papa was almost a bleeder, the doctors said, and we in the family knew this. He walked to the doctor's office, three blocks away, leaving a trail of blood, and sat with his foot propped on a chair while Dr. Haynes sewed the gash. Trailing along with him, I watched, fascinated, while the needle pushed through the tough skin. Not once did Papa wince. I winced for him. The bandage in place, Papa walked home, still fuming about the fool who first of all drank demon rum, then broke bottles in a swimming place. The pain was ignored in favor of his hate for liquor. Next Sunday the incident furnished part of his sermon.

23

To Evansville

THE second summer we were in Calhoun, Mama and Papa decided to take me to Evansville, Indiana, one of the terminal points for the packets that plied the rivers from there to Bowling Green. I had never been out of the state and was excited over the prospect.

Two passenger boats, the *Bowling Green* and *Evansville*, furnished almost the only transportation between the two cities for which they were named. Their route was from Barren River through Green River to the mouth of the Ohio. Excitement filled the day before our scheduled trip, for it was impossible to set the exact time of the boat's arrival because of the delays in loading and unloading freight. The lower deck was used for this, and also for taking passengers aboard at specified points along the river.

At least twelve hours before leaving we were ready to rush down to the landing. Clean and dressed except for our top clothes and Sunday shoes, we slept fitfully that night, listening for the far-off whistle that would tell of the boat's arrival. The pilots accommodatingly gave loud warning blasts as they approached from miles down the river.

Papa's stockinged feet came padding into my room. "The whistle, Willard! Get up, the boat's coming!"

Quickly adding a dress and shoes to my attire, I ran

a brush over my hair, picked up my purse with the silver dollar I'd earned selling some fryers I'd raised, and went outside. Mama, Papa, and I walked to the landing in the semidarkness. The river shimmered under a pale fading moon as we watched the bend for a first glimpse of smoke above the trees. We listened for the blast that signaled the opening of the locks below Calhoun, which would set our boat in lower water. A dam which crossed at this point kept the water higher on our side.

It came, three short blasts, the signal for men to take their places on the high lock walls, ready to turn huge wheels which opened or shut the heavy gates. It was even more fun going to Evansville, for we went through two locks on the way.

As the boat turned ashore, barefoot deck hands, stripped to the waist, ran up the gangplank while it was still in midair and rode it down to the shore. They ran to pick up the freight and luggage, chanting as they went. Some large bales were handled by several hands, who timed their efforts with what sounded to me like "hump now, hump now, HUMP!"—the last "hump" giving impetus to the initial lifting of the weight.

We went aboard, climbing the narrow stairway to the second, or passenger, deck. We stowed our luggage in a narrow stateroom, went back to the deck, and sat in chairs at the front, watching the turmoil of the water and feeling the throb of the engines as the pilot backed the *Bowling Green* away from the landing.

Slowly, the pilot steered the *Bowling Green* into the narrow opening in the lock walls. The gate was closed, and we could feel our boat lowering itself into the box-like space. When only the lock wall itself could be seen, the lower gate opened, as men on the wall turned huge wheels frantically. The *Bowling Green*, with a parting blast, brought her huge bulk outside.

When we were on our way in the middle of the river, I began to wander around the deck and into the salon. Each side had doors leading into small staterooms with upper and lower berths, and at the back were the kitchen and restrooms. Unable to wait longer, I ventured into the toilet. It was a rather frightening experience to look into the toilet seat and see the huge paddle wheel threshing white foam beneath you. For small children who might be frightened by the sight and noise there was a slopjar which I rather timidly considered using, shuddering at the thought of falling through the hole and landing between the big wheels, which would carry me round and round until I fell into the river. Scornfully, I rejected the foolish idea. After all, an eleven-year-old girl was not a baby. I climbed aboard one of the seats, which felt rather large, but holding on tightly, I gave over to the rhythm of the wheel and the throbbing of the motors.

At breakfast time a long table was let up in the center of the salon. A cloth tablecloth covered it, and two waiters in white coats set it with heavy plates, silver, and enormous starched napkins rolled into tricorners and stuck into water glasses by each plate.

People were coming out of the staterooms now, for the smell of breakfast began to seep from the galley—good smells, for river chefs were famous for their cooking. At the sound of the ship's bell, we sat at the table, and the captain, in full dress, took his place at the head.

The day passed quickly, though there were no other children aboard on this trip. Four people sat at a small table on deck playing a game with spot cards, and I wondered if the prettiest woman was "bad." Her partner in the game was handsome—maybe he was a gambler. I pondered this quite a while, thinking that good-looking people should be immune to sin; only ugly ones should have guilt.

As we stopped at a landing spot, I heard an awful roar, and wondered if some cow were protesting being taken aboard the boat. Three deck hands were forcing the most hideous man I ever saw up the gangplank. One on each side pulled an arm, while another pushed his bulk from the back. I crept close to Papa. "Will they bring him up here?" I asked.

Papa tried to hide a smile at my fear. "His mother is with him," he pointed out. "She won't let him hurt you."

As they brought him to the upper deck I got a closer look.

His face was covered with a bright red beard, stiff and curly. His tongue lolled from his open mouth from side to side, and when his mother told Papa and Mama later on that he'd been "marked" by a dying calf, I believed her, for once I'd seen a calf's mouth and it looked just like the man's. To prove her point, the mother took one of her son's hands, for he was quiet now except for some continuous rumbling sounds, and showed his fingernails, shaped like a calf's hoof. I stayed close to Papa or Mama until they got off at the next landing.

That night in the top bunk of the small stateroom I was too excited to sleep. I could look out of the small porthole and see the land sliding by. It seemed as if we were still, except for the rhythmic throbbing of the engines, and the land itself was moving. For awhile I thought about it until I fell asleep.

It was still dark when Papa awakened me, with his usual "Time all honest folks were out of bed!"

Sleepily I dressed and we went to the front deck where we sat watching the deck below. The captain came out, holding a large bottle in one hand and a small glass in the other. The deck hands gathered around eagerly as he poured each one a drink. Suddenly the captain looked up and saw Papa.

"I'm sorry, Brother Cherry, but this is the only way I can get men to come aboard and work." His tone was an apology to a minister who preached often against the evils of whiskey.

Papa took a look around to gather his thoughts, I supposed, then said a little condescendingly, "Well, if it's the only way—" and left the opinion dangling in the air.

I looked at Papa in surprise and wondered how he'd approach "Demon Rum" in his next sermon. I'd sure listen to see how he handled *that*.

Arriving in Evansville right after breakfast, we climbed the hill to the main street and began to look for a place to eat our lunch. I stopped and pointed to a sign which read:

THE ACME HOTEL—Evansville, Indiana
Rates 50¢, 75¢, $1.00 a day
Jug orders promptly filled.

I think the last words of the sign stopped Papa, for we went on down the street until we came to a more respectable restaurant, where we sat at a cloth-covered table and examined the menus the waitress brought us. I marveled at the coldness of the glass of water she set by our plates. It had pieces of ice floating in it, and I wondered if I could take one out for a bite without Mama's stopping me. Mama always seemed to know what I was thinking, so I unfolded the large stiff napkin beside my plate and took a look at the menu instead. There were too many choices, everything from fried chicken to roast beef, and thirty-five cents would buy the meat, three vegetables, a drink, and dessert. Mama let me have iced tea, and didn't say anything when I took bits of ice out with my spoon and chewed them.

We visited the stores in the afternoon, watching to see that we didn't lose sight of the time our boat was to leave the pier.

I couldn't believe the size of these stores; we were used to two counters at the most, running the length of one room. We went from one archway to another, and found that rooms were divided to display shoes, dresses, children's clothes, yard goods, and other items.

We went to the yard goods department and Mama began to look for a piece of material for my winter dress. The weather was still very warm, and I was inclined to favor the lighter dotted swisses or lacy-all-over embroidery. Mama felt some heavier material, held the color against my face and red hair, and let me see how it looked in the mirror that covered the wall almost from ceiling to floor.

We decided that brown was my best color, and as the clerk cut off the yardage, I thrilled to know that this winter I wouldn't be wearing one of my sisters' dresses cut down to my size. Every Sunday I'd be as well dressed as the rest of my friends.

Mama had already bought my school clothes for the winter. All my girl friends had decided we'd wear middy blouses and skirts, and Mama had made two serge skirts for me, one dark blue, one brown, with long-sleeved cotton middies to match. There was also a ready-made white middy, trimmed with braid, for special occasions. With the high-topped button shoes we had (white buckskin with tassels), there would be no question about being stylish that year. Mama made one more purchase: a pair of woolen gloves. My coat from the winter before would be about right this year, since Mama had allowed for growth when she bought it.

Papa had warned us to watch out for pickpockets in a city the size of Evansville, so I walked down the street clutching my purse in both arms, watching to see that no slinky thief darted out of a dark doorway and snatched my worldly goods. It was a kind of adventure. I was almost disappointed when nothing happened.

We were tired when we walked back to the river to get on the boat and go home. Supper was to be served aboard, and we saw a grocery wagon pull up and unload baskets of food. I wondered what we'd have for supper; it would be good. The packets were noted for serving good meals.

After supper, we sat on the upper deck in comfortable chairs, listening to the water as the big paddles behind the *Bowling Green* churned it into foam. The deck hands sat or lay on the lower deck, and one of them started to sing in his untrained, beautiful voice:

I looked over Jordan and what did I see
Comin' for to carry me home?

As the song went on, I looked over the Ohio River, and thought sleepily that the *Bowling Green* made a wonderful chariot to carry me home. I thought of the dress goods Mama had bought for me, and felt grateful that she had shared the pin money she and I had saved from selling June apples, fresh eggs, and vegetables from Papa's garden.

Other voices joined the first one, and I wondered how any band of angels could ever sing a sweeter song than the deckhands were singing below.

24

Chapels

CHAPEL was an integral part of our school in Calhoun. Devotional services were held in each classroom at the beginning of the day. The last Friday in the month all the grades were marched into the auditorium to be treated to a lecture by some local celebrity, followed by a special program by one grade.

Whenever there was a protracted meeting being held in the town, the visiting evangelist was guest of honor, and we were offered each preacher's special belief as well as an invitation to attend the nightly service held in the church.

Papa was often the chosen guest for the school's

Every deed of today,
Every thought gone astray,
Every time I've been tempted and failed to say "Nay,"
I recall in the still of the night,
As I lie on my pillow tonight.

Songs like this were considered good therapy, and being reminded of our sins was a regular part of our training. The song returned to haunt me many nights as I remembered my failings and resolved, as sleep overtook me, that tomorrow would be better.

Recitations were a part of our program. It was my turn to perform. We were encouraged to emote to our heart's content. My favorite elocutionist was my Aunt Bess T.C. Cherry, who taught the art in college. My ambition was to emulate her. I spent hours before our cracked mirror trying out gestures, pursing my lips for a proper enunciation, and bringing tears to my eyes at the proper time.

Today I had chosen the poem, "Send Them to Bed with a Kiss," a ballad about a child who had been naughty and was sent to bed in disgrace. He, of course, died in the night, and when I noticed a woman weeping in the audience I, proud of my histrionic ability, emoted harder, causing her to sob aloud. Later on, my pride took a hard fall when I learned she had recently lost a child. My conscience warred with my pride for a long, long time as I lay on my pillow that night. The war ended as I realized that I hadn't known or intended to hurt her. My guilt was supplanted by satisfaction in my ability to move others (I'd seen several mothers wipe a tear away during my recitation) and I was relieved.

Our program ended with a drill. There were some

who argued that this might be the first step toward dancing in the schools. Dancing was of the devil. This was one of the few doctrines agreed upon by all the denominations in our town—Methodist, Baptist, and Christian. Such a wedge of Satan would never be permitted in the schools.

We stood sedately, holding wands covered with white crepe paper, tipped with a silver star, and formed patterns on the stage, many like the Virginia Reel and square dances, except that our feet stepped firmly on the floor. We knew that we were beautiful, and the applause that came from our audience indicated a very satisfactory "well done." For a few minutes we had been prima donnas and leading men, and I wondered how I could ever bear descending from clouds of glory and treading Calhoun's plank walks again.

25

Ox in the Ditch

CALHOUN often had spring floods before the huge dams were built to stop the devastating overflow. When time came for them, people in the low lying areas simply moved to higher ground and waited for the water to recede.

But the flood in the year 1911 was not one to wait out. It came with a mighty rush that trapped people and animals. Sometimes a rooster and a fox would be seen riding the same piece of wood to safety, and much fresh meat was obtained by boys in boats removing rabbits and squirrels from floating logs.

Few household goods were saved. Most people fled their houses in the clothes they wore; some escaped in night clothes only. Boats plied up and down the river day and night trying to rescue those stranded by high water.

The courthouse was turned into a refugee center, and every house on high ground was opened to those who needed shelter. We took in a family of five, the Scotts, and Mama turned over two rooms to them and allowed them to use her kitchen. The government sent in food supplies, rank bacon (I can smell it cooking now, and wondered where such meat came from), dark flour, molasses, and dried beans.

Sometimes at night I visited the family as they sat around the fire in their room and talked of the things they had lost. There had been plenty of meat cured for the year, but as the water went down and the man was able to get some of it out of his smokehouse, he found it had been waterlogged and ruined. They did bring home one aged ham, which their old hound seemed to relish anyhow.

At the beginning of the flood, we heard a loud knock on our door early one Sunday morning. A man stood there, wet and muddy. Twins had been born during the storm that night and the mother and babies had been removed by boat to a house on an island nearby.

"She ain't doin' so good," the man told Papa. After all, everyone came to the preacher for help in all kinds of trouble.

Papa turned to Mama. "Come on, let's go." Mama gathered up a few things and put them into a bag.

"I want to come, too," I began. Papa just nodded "yes" and we were on our way.

The man untied a boat from a tree near the shore and we got in. He rowed us to a house that stood in the center of the water, which had reached almost to the front steps.

We went into the house and on a bed in the corner lay a very young woman, pale and ill. I looked for the babies and found them lying on a pillow in a rocker near the fire. Such tiny creatures—they hardly looked human, and they made small mewling noises. Mama put one of them into my arms. It felt cold and clammy and I held it close, trying to give it some of my warmth.

Mama warmed some milk (she had brought a bottle along with her from home), but when she tried to feed the babies from a spoon they sputtered it out of their mouths. They couldn't seem to swallow.

"They need warm clothes, Papa," Mama told him. "Go tell Mr. Cline to open up his store and give you some outing flannel."

"On Sunday?" I thought. Stores were never open on Sunday.

Mama took clean towels and wrapped the babies. She warmed a brick by the fire and wrapped it well and put it under the pillow in the chair.

"I'll be back as soon as I can," she told the father.

When we got home Mama opened the sewing machine. She took the flannel from Papa and began to cut out tiny gowns and tear off diapers.

"You can run up the seams on the machine," she told me.

"On Sunday? Aren't we going to church?" I asked.

Mama shook her head, and I sewed away, enjoying this unheard-of experience of treadling the machine on Sunday—and skipping services, as a bonus.

Papa must have cut his sermon short that day, for it was only a little past twelve when we went back to the twins. He must have told about the need, too, for while we were there, food, bedding, and warm clothes were brought in. Mama let me dress one of the twins, and as I held the baby it felt even colder than it had that morning. It had a funny color, too, and as I sat rocking it, it gave a tiny lurch and lay still. Mama came and took it out of my arms. She laid it gently by the side of its twin, took my hand, which she did not do often, and led me from the room. She didn't have to tell me that the baby had died in my arms.

I wondered why life was so sad at times, and why such tiny things had to suffer so. I thought of little naked birds falling from their nests to die, and remembered the verse Papa quoted to me when I once asked him why: "For we know that all creation groaneth and travaileth in pain together until now" (Rom. 8:22).

Later in the week the water was still high but less turbulent. One afternoon Papa took me to the river's edge and we got into a flat-bottomed boat. He took up the oars and rowed to Rumsey, the town across the river from Calhoun.

All I could see was a stretch of water. It looked endless, with only the top of a tree or building extending upward. He rowed toward a small store, built as many were then, with a door front and back and a counter on each side. The water came almost to the tops of the counters.

"You're going to have an experience you never had before," he told me, chuckling as he did when he found something very amusing. He laid the oars alongside the boat and, holding on to the counters, brought us inside. Dress goods filled the higher shelves on the right, and canned things the grocery side. Nothing had been disturbed—nobody would think of looting and thereby taking advantage of a bad situation like the flood. There had already been trouble enough. So we rowed through the front door, then through the back.

"I'm glad the river is going down, Papa," I said. "But what will people do now?"

"Same as they always have," Papa told me. "The ones with any get-up will scrape the mud off their things and thank the Lord it adds fertility to the soil. The ones who are no account will find another good excuse not to work another year."

"I heard the twins died," I said as we rowed toward home. I hadn't wanted to say the words but this seemed the right place to get them off my chest.

Papa nodded, "Death is not always cruel," he explained. "They are in a happy place, and if they had lived, they might not have always been." (I remembered this a year later when we had a family death and reminded Papa of what he had said.)

"By the way, Papa, what was the subject of your sermon last Sunday?" It was the first time I'd thought about it during the week.

"'When the Ox Is in the Ditch, Pull Him Out,' of course. You know you don't sew on Sunday unless he is?" Papa had a rather anxious look. His eyes twinkled then and he said with a smile, reading my mind, I suppose:

"Just you be sure you don't push him in on Saturday night."

26

Katherine

THE year 1910 ushered in a new way of life for all of the Cherry family. The people in Calhoun were beginning to like having Papa for their minister, and offerings came in, both in food and money, in a satisfactory way. Mary was married, David and Nell were teaching. Katherine and Elizabeth were attending Logan Female College. They had been left behind when we moved from Russellville after a lot of discussion. Papa feared that without his counsel to guide them, they might be led astray. But Mama pointed out to him the strict way girls at Logan were treated. They were not allowed to go to town without having a teacher for a chaperone. It was quite an ordinary sight to see several girls, dressed in their caps and gowns, walking two by two, enter a store and wait while one of them made a purchase. Logan girls were never allowed to appear in public out of uniform. Once a month, the boys who attended Bethel College across town were permitted to visit the Logan girls for two hours. This visit took place in the huge reception room on the first floor on Sunday afternoon. The room was a dark, formal place, with chairs arranged around the walls. Heavy drapes almost obscured the long, narrow windows. Kerosene lamps gave off filtered colors through the flowered globes, set in strategic places. No chance here, Mama pointed out, for a girl to be alone with a boy.

In the fall of 1910 when Papa took Katherine and Elizabeth back to enter college after spending the summer at home, he took me with him. I was allowed to spend the night in the dormitory in Katherine and Elizabeth's room which they shared with two other girls. It had two double beds, a dresser with four drawers, a washstand with a bowl and pitcher, and room for four towels and washcloths to hang across a bar at the top. A decorated slopjar was concealed behind a door in the bottom of the washstand. This the four girls took turns emptying every morning after they had poured their wash water from the bowl into it.

Mama had sent a big box of food to the girls, so after curfew, which came a half hour after the girls returned from study hall downstairs, several of the other girls in rooms down the corridor were invited in for a midnight feast. I shared their secrecy as they whispered quietly so that the teacher who monitored the floor would not get an inkling about what was going on. All of us, I'm sure, felt a delightful sense of wickedness.

Katherine had brought Dick, her canary, with her to college, and the next morning she let it get out of the cage. It promptly flew out of the window. After she caught it, she asked me to take it home with me and keep it for her. So, very proudly, I carried the bird in its cage with me on the train home.

I hated to tell Katherine goodbye. She had always been my best friend—one who never told on me, whatever I did wrong. She would, instead, sit down by me and "talk it out," and many times I'd decide to change my ways. Katherine was so beautiful. Sometimes I envied her hair. It was dark auburn, and she wore it in a long braid which fell into three long curls at the end. Her eyes were a deep brown. Her skin was fair, marred only by a few freckles. Katherine was tall and slender, and I was prone to brag about her accomplishment as an athlete. The Logan girls had a volleyball team, and Katherine was captain. She was popular everywhere she lived. She was voted "most graceful" in the college yearbook.

Katherine was especially close to Papa. He often told about the way she would leave her playmates when she was small and run to meet him. She would take his hand and rub her cheek against it, something which none of the other girls ever did, I'm sure. Mama often said she was the nearest substitute for Roxy Papa had.

Bad news was waiting for us when Papa and I got home. Grandma Cherry had fallen and broken her hip, and Grandfather George had asked Mama to come to the farm for awhile and nurse her. This would bring about several complications. My parents didn't think I was mature enough to keep the house going when Mama left, so they decided to call Katherine and ask her to come home and stay while Mama was gone. Being Katherine, she said she would, and Mama left for Bowling Green.

Katherine always liked to do housework, and she took a lot of pride in keeping the parsonage. One afternoon there arrived at the house a delegation from the Ladies' Aid Society, who announced that they felt called upon to examine the parsonage (since it was really their duty to see that it was well kept), and proceeded to do this. Katherine's face was very red, I noticed. It surprised me to see her angry, but she said nothing. The ladies walked into the kitchen, and when one of them, whom I secretly called "Mrs. Nosey," went to the piesafe, opened the door, and raised the cover of a dish, Katherine made a sputtering sound and ran outside. This left me alone, since Papa was away at the time, and having few inhibitions, I said sarcastically, "I hope it suits you! Katherine is the cleanest person I know. Would you like to have her come to your house and clean up some of your mess?"

The ladies gasped, looked at each other, and shook their heads. I didn't worry about being told on, either, for I knew that they had chosen a time for their inspection when Papa was gone. They knew he would not have appreciated their intrusion.

Katherine was crying when she came inside after they left, and she didn't stop me as I fumed and scolded to Papa when he came in. He put his arm around Katherine and said, "I hope I'll live to see the day when preachers and their families are not considered public property. Some time preachers will get a steady income and live like other people. If church members would only tithe this would happen soon."

Mama stayed with Grandma a month, then Papa decided that she should come home, and that Katherine would take her place, since Grandma was better. Again Katherine consented and spent the rest of the winter at the farm. This caused her to miss a year in college and so she had to repeat her graduation year. Papa often suffered over the consequences of her added year at Logan. "If she could have finished last year." Tears would fill his eyes as he remembered what happened.

Two weeks before the following Christmas, Mama came to the table with a pained looked on her face. It had to be pained for Papa to notice it, but he did and asked, "Mammy, you aren't sick, are you?"

"I had a terrible dream last night," she said.

"Tell us," I urged eagerly. Mama's dreams had a way of coming true. She had dreamed on the night he was born that my sister Mary had a baby boy, and they lived in Alabama! The next day when the telephone rang to give us the message, Mama wasn't surprised at all. "What did you dream?" I urged.

"I saw Katherine in a gray plush coffin. She was wearing her green silk dress piped in pink. I know she's sick." Mama pushed aside her plate of uneaten food, went to the phone, and cranked the bell. "I want Logan Female College in Russellville," she told Central. "It's urgent."

While Central was getting the number I could see the campus covered with snow, and the holly trees with their red berries outlined against it.

When the connection was made, Mama said, "I want to ask about Katherine Cherry. Is she all right?"

The answer brought a look of alarm to Mama's face. "I'm coming to bring her home," she said, and hung up. She turned to Papa, "Katherine is sick. There is an epidemic of typhoid fever. Several of the girls are sick."

We learned later that the source of the disease was drinking water from the cistern which was near the dormitory. Some of the girls had emptied slopjars too near, they found, instead of carrying them to the hole which had been dug farther away for this purpose.

Mama left next day and returned two days later with Katherine. Papa and I met the boat at the landing. He had hired a two-horse carriage, which excited me because of the ride and Katherine's return. I had a surprise for her, too. Knowing how she liked fried chicken, I had raised some fryers late that fall and kept them to share with her at Christmas.

When she was helped off the boat, I told her about my surprise. She laid a hand on my shoulder and said, "Sorry, honey, I don't think I'll ever eat them, but you were good to save them for me."

When we got home she lay on a cot that Papa had set up in the best front room. He called Dr. Haynes, who left the room after examining her, shaking his head. "That dumb doctor at the college! He gave the girls calomel! Purging's the last thing anyone with typhoid fever needs."

We nursed Katherine night and day. David, Nell, and Elizabeth came home before the holiday and took turns sitting with her. Katherine lost so much weight, and looked so pale. In her light sleep she moaned in pain. One afternoon I was left to sit by her while the others rested. I thought she was asleep, but she opened her eyes and smiled at me. "Willard, read me the fourteenth chapter of John," she said.

I opened her small Bible which she always kept nearby and started to show how well I could read, but the first words brought tears, and, my voice choking, I read, "Let not your heart be troubled, Ye believe in God, believe also in me. In my father's house are many mansions. . . ." My voice broke and I laid my head on the cot beside her and sobbed. Katherine put a thin hand on my head and her fingers passed back and forth over the back of my neck the way they did when I had been hurt or felt sick.

"Don't cry, Willard," she said softly. "Read the next verse."

My eyes swam with tears. "If it were not so I would have told you. I go to prepare a place for you."

"I'm going ahead, Willard, but I'll save a place for your mansion beside mine." I was crying so hard now that Mama awakened and came into the room. She motioned for me to leave the room and I went outside and picked up my pet chicken. I held him in my arms and cried into his feathers. Life was too hard to bear sometimes. Without Katherine a big part of me would be gone. Finally I went into the house and opened Papa's big Bible. I turned to the same chapter and finished the next verse, which brought me some comfort. "And if I go and prepare a place for you, I will come again and receive you unto myself, that where I am, there ye may be also."

The day before Christmas Eve Dr. Haynes suggested that we give Katherine her gifts early. Her boyfriend and all the other young men in Katherine's crowd had decided to give their girls a gold-handled umbrella with their initials engraved on the top of the handle. Papa invited him to join us when she got her presents. I had bought Katherine a little green gum drop frog with beady eyes. She laughed when she took it into her hand and begged for a bite. Since all food was limited for typhoid patients, Papa refused to let her have it. Afterwards he regretted it, he often told us.

Not long after she got her gifts she began to hemorrhage. Dr. Haynes was delivering a baby in the country, and it was impossible for him to come.

Katherine began to suffer so much that we finally got a dentist to come to the house and give her a shot of morphine. It was early afternoon and she had almost stopped breathing. Several friends had come in, as was the custom. I stood in the doorway and saw the blood which had saturated the top bedclothes. Turning, I ran to our next door neighbor's house. She was rocking before her fire. I ran to her and she took me into her lap, big girl that I was, and held me.

"Katherine's dying," I sobbed. "She's dying!"

"Yes, I know," Mrs. Little comforted me. "Not many people live when they have typhoid. Katherine didn't have a chance—what with the calomel and moving her so far."

That night as Katherine lay in her casket, Mama stood looking at her. "She looks just like she did in my dream."

Katherine's boyfriend picked up the umbrella he had brought her. He was weeping. "She will never use it now," he told me. Friends from all the churches came by that night. One old man who came had loved Katherine dearly because she always stopped by on her way to town to speak to him. His wrinkled face, which had always looked hard to me, was broken now. Tears ran down his cheeks unashamedly, and his bony old body was wracked by sobs. "She always treated me like I was kin."

The next day the family carried Katherine to Bowling Green to be buried. Elizabeth stayed with me and kept me busy all day helping to clean and disinfect the house. One special job she had me do was wash all the doors and knobs with carbolic acid water. Before Papa left he had taken the cot and all the bedclothes out to the garden and burned them. I could not stand seeing the flames and I hid my face in a pillow. Even the things Katherine had touched were gone, I realized. It was my saddest and loneliest Christmas Eve.

Katherine, my dearest friend, had left me to wait alone for a dreary Christmas, ushered in without my family, except for Elizabeth. She had decided that very day to forsake teaching (an approved profession for women) for nursing, an occupation few decent girls dared to embrace. Her choice, when revealed, caused raised eyebrows and the shaking of heads.

Katherine's death also brought another decision in the family. Nell decided to go to Patterson, N.J., enroll in Blake Business College, and become secretary, which also caused some tongue clicking.

I decided never again to love anyone. Love could hurt too much. I'd live aloof from any emotional involvement. Dick, Katherine's canary, was cheeping at me, trying to get me to answer him. I cleaned his cage, gave him fresh food and water, and we talked awhile. How I wished for a dog or cat to hold! Something I could touch and feel! Papa had a big "NO!" for that.

Restlessly I went outside and started walking down the street. My pet rooster followed me and I walked so far he got tired and flew up on my shoulder.

I cuddled my cheek against his feathers. That pet chicken was my most comforting friend.

27

Calliope Time

EVERY summer in Calhoun we looked forward to one major event, the arrival of the showboat.

For a week or so we read posters advertising "MAGNIFICENT ACTS THAT HAVE BEEN PERFORMED BEFORE THE CROWNED HEADS OF EUROPE," and the excitement was almost too much to be endured as we imagined the treats depicted on the colorful pictures. We waited impatiently.

Then one glorious day, there it was! The sound of music so thrilling that even grownups, whom we youngsters judged past caring for such frivolity, stopped their whittling or rocking and listened.

Was there ever such a robust sound as "Listen to the Mocking Bird" pealing forth as the showboat approached the locks below Calhoun?

We ran to the river and watched the boat, the *New Sensation*, as it came to shore. Close up we could see the man on the top deck working the big calliope. His ears were covered with thick muffs, for the music was deafening. Puffs of steam escaped the pipes as he pressed each huge key. One of my friends who lived three miles away said she heard it too and recognized the tune.

The people on the upper deck didn't look like the ones who had been advertised to do the acts we had read about, such as globe rolling, magic, and ventriloquism. I decided that they were inside, and was surprised when one of the men sweeping the deck turned out to be the hypnotist. I recognized him by his beard during his act.

When the roustabouts lay down on the lower deck to sleep, there was no more activity to be seen. I ran home, remembering that this was Wednesday night, prayer meeting time, and fearing that Papa would say "no" to visiting the showboat. I didn't have Mr. Browder in this town to persuade him to allow me to sample the world's temptations.

It was with some pride and a little comfort that I reminded myself it wouldn't cost Papa anything for my admission. Elizabeth had promised to take me. She had taught in the local school the year before (I was one of her pupils, and I'd hated it) and brought home the huge salary of thirty dollars a month. She had saved most of it for her entrance into nurses' training that fall. I was proud that she would pay our admission in actual money, for eggs, slabs of bacon, chickens, corn meal, fresh vegetables, butter, or milk were also accepted. It gave me a sense of superiority to know we would walk up to the cashier nonchalantly and pay our quarters.

Papa hesitated awhile before saying we could go, with the stipulation that we would attend prayer meeting first. Since the show started at eight o'clock, we'd have plenty of time if Papa didn't prolong his service—and if we ran to the boat as soon as prayer meeting was over.

Out of breath, we walked across the wide gangplank of the boat *New Sensation*. The gas lights almost put out my eyes, glittering and lighting the ripples on the water in the river. I saw one of my schoolmates chasing a rooster across the deck. His fare had gotten loose, and I felt disdainful at such a plebeian way of paying an admission fee.

We took our seats near the front. I saw a few unfriendly stares from one of Papa's members and his family. They seemed to question me, "Why are preacher's kids here on prayer meeting night?" Silently I answered, "At least I went to church first. You didn't."

The lights were turned down and the show started with a man in minstrel array who did a soft shoe dance and sang. A girl dressed in a slinky silver gown and a peacock headdress sang a plaintive song about a lost love which brought sniffs and blowing of noses. There were other acts, too, but the final one gave me food for thought for days. A man hypnotized a pretty girl and suspended her in midair with only one arm resting in the center of a cut-out broom.

Sleep was late in coming that night as I considered slipping onto the showboat and beginning my career as a featured performer aboard the *New Sensation*.

Perhaps the fear that I might be hypnotized caused me to abandon that idea, so instead I snuggled down in my bed, anticipating the fishing trip Papa had promised the next day.

28

Jeffersontown

THE Louisville Conference's annual meeting each October was always exciting. We knew that four years was the longest time we could ever stay in one place. So when Papa left for the conference in 1914 we knew that since our time was up in Calhoun, another move was coming. We waited anxiously to hear what the new town would be.

I had decided that my name, Willard, would have to be changed to Frances at the next town we lived in. There would be no way to do this in Calhoun where I was known as Willard by so many people. I hated the name for some unclear reason and always had, since the first time I recognized it as mine.

One morning before we moved I announced at breakfast that from that moment on I'd refuse to answer when Papa or Mama called me Willard. Only Frances would be noticed. This continued to be my policy until Frances came easily from my parents.

When Papa came home from the conference he told us we would be going to Jeffersontown, fifteen miles from Louisville, and I was excited over the idea of moving to a place near Kentucky's largest city. In Jeffersontown I would be introduced to my new friends as Frances.

The four years in Calhoun had been such happy

ones after the first few dreadful months. I hated to leave Green River, the two country churches, and my friends. We left on the mail boat to take the train at Livermore to Louisville, arriving there after dark, too late to take the streetcar that ran from Louisville to Jeffersontown.

We looked around at the hotels near the station, and found one advertising a reasonable fee for a night. We registered and, since we had not eaten, walked into the dining room. When we looked at the menu we were dumbfounded. The prices were much too high for Papa's pocketbook. He decided on one of the less expensive items and Mama and I ordered bowls of soup, at the enormous price of twenty-five cents each.

It was my first time to spend a night in a hotel in a big city, and it was hard going to sleep with streetcars clanking up and down the street, lights flashing into the windows. Life in Louisville continued through the night like it was still day!

The next morning we went down for breakfast and when we read the menu we discovered that every on it was priced higher than twenty-five cents. Papa scratched his head and said, "Why don't you order another bowl of soup?" Mama and I vetoed that suggestion, choosing a bowl of oatmeal instead, at thirty cents.

The trip to Jeffersontown was my first ride on a streetcar. Traveling on trains had always made Mama sick, and the streetcar did the same. When we got off, it took awhile before we could walk to the parsonage, only one block from the terminal.

We had lived in such different kinds of places that we had mixed feelings about the sort of house that

154

would be ours next. The Jeffersontown parsonage was built near the street. It was a two-story wooden affair with a small front porch and large rooms. It was in good repair, and when we went inside we found the last family had left it in good condition. The furniture was adequate until our things came later on. Mama sent me to the store on the square and I chose Mr. Finelli's grocery at which to buy food. He was Italian, I heard later, the first foreigner I'd ever met. While I picked out my groceries I listened in fascination as he talked to his wife. She was turning an ice cream freezer at one side of the store. The language was strange, but it sounded happy. I discovered that they kept three kinds of homemade ice cream on hand, and cones were priced from one cent to a nickel, which gave a choice of three kinds if you were lucky enough to have three cents. We became good friends, the Finellis and I.

When I got home from the store I looked over the house and decided to take the room back of Mama's and Papa's, which was two steps lower than theirs, with a second stairway coming up from the living room below. The ceiling in my room was sloped on each side. There were dormer windows and a Franklin heater at one end. It was a cozy place, and I felt at once that it was mine.

The parsonage was on the main street in Jeffersontown. The houses nearby had been built long ago, and showed evidence that years had taken their toll. One brick house across the street was built on the sidewalk like the Browders' in Russellville, and for a moment I wished that I could be a child, back with Harriet again.

That afternoon Papa and I walked down the street to the church, which was almost two blocks away. It was a large brick structure and somewhat forbidding in its austerity. We went inside and found it in good repair, clean, but to me, unwelcoming. I liked his country appointment (Cooper's Chapel which we saw later) much better.

When we reached the square Papa asked where the school was located. We walked down a side street and at the end we found a wooden building with two rooms. Through the open windows I could see children of different sizes and ages sitting at double desks, and could hear the school teacher (a man!) yelling. I didn't look forward to education in that place. We learned that each room had four grades, and since I was used to only two grades in my room in Calhoun, I wondered how all the noise would affect me.

Next day my worst fears were realized. The teacher, who had a white mustache and white hair and was dressed immaculately, held a long hickory switch in his hand and used it on the back of anyone, girl or boy, who angered him—which seemed to me easy to do. Most of the students mumbled aloud while studying. I made up my mind that first day to talk to Papa about letting me go to another school.

Papa inquired around and after awhile found a country school which I could attend—St. Matthews (also two rooms)—a few miles down the streetcar track. It was a seven month school instead of the usual eight. Every morning I rode the trolley to the school, and back home at night. St. Matthews was a German settlement, and the boys and girls were all of German descent. The extra month was spent on crops on the farms. Every moment was precious and every cent protected. The lunches they brought were so delicious that I traded any of my store-bought things for one of their biscuits and sausage. I loved the school and Miss Bryant, our teacher.

There were three of us in my class studying for the eighth grade county examination which was given in Louisville every year at the courthouse. Having arrived late, I had only three months to prepare. It was a big day when Joe, William, and I rode the streetcar to Louisville and sat in the big auditorium taking the test. At noon we were allowed to go out for lunch, but we were too nervous to eat. Miss Bryant had spent a lot of time coaching us for the test. We passed, and since high schools in Louisville were either for boys or girls, Joe, William, and I had no more contact with each other.

Papa had always resented the attitudes many church members had about paying their minister. He had been making notes for years on the tithe law and it was in Jeffersontown in 1915 that he finally got his book ready to be published by the Pentecostal Publishing Company. Everywhere he had preached, tithing had been one of his themes, and in most places he ha[d] persuaded some of his members to give a tenth to the church. In places where they had, we had fared far better. The churches and parsonages were upgraded and times had been more pleasant.

Doing research on his book, *The Tithe Law*, Papa found that little had ever been written on the subject. So it was from the Bible itself that he got most of his data. He felt a keen distaste for the humiliating way most preachers were paid. He wrote in his book, "The fact is we have money for everything except the church of God. . .worse still under our present regime these scrappy collections which is a mere pittance of the tithe. . . are the mere bits and bones of our income from which we have devoured the meat. . . . No well-bred, high toned, and self-respecting man can commit his destiny to such a system of uncertainty and beggary without an agony of great self-denial. . . . So our only escape is. . . taking the tithe law as the basis upon which to disburse all our temporary possessions."

The Tithe Law may not have been a financial success, but many people were blessed by following its advice, and many ministers were encouraged to preach more openly on the subject which had heretofore been off limits. Papa had accumulated some money now, but when Mama heard that he was planning to have 5000 copies of his book published at his own expense, she argued, "But, Papa, we were saving for the time we retire in Elkton!"

"Now, Mammy," Papa's voice was confident, "I'll get enough from the sale of the book to make almost twice as much. I'm asking thirty-five cents a copy, and that adds up!"

Mama sighed and started humming almost under her breath, "His grace is enough. . . ." (The book didn't sell well enough to pay back the thousand dollars, so we added more books to our moving list.)

There were no young people my age nearby in Jeffersontown, so my spare time was spent with older folks. One family in our church, the Stuckeys, consisted of a widow, her two daughters, and her son, who was a doctor. The Stuckeys and I walked to church and prayer meeting together, and I spent summer mornings in their upstairs sitting room talking or playing games. They were entertaining and they always welcomed me. As was the custom, on Sunday afternoons all of us went for a walk and usually a young man—the younger girl's beau—joined us. The widow's granddaughter from Louisville, who was usually kept home to take care of her invalid mother, sometimes visited and came along too. She was my age and I felt sorry for her because of the dull and sad life she led. We must have made a rare sight as we walked down the streets, the widow in her black dress and long black veil, the older girl always in black, the younger one with little more color in her attire. We walked sedately, two by two, saying little. It must have been quite a procession, with the doctor, alone, bringing up the rear.

There were lots of Baptists in Jeffersontown. Papa had become more lenient in his attitude toward them after his experience in Calhoun, but when a young Baptist minister from the seminary in Louisville visited one Saturday in Jeffersontown and invited me to play tennis with him, Papa drew a line. I was not yet sixteen, so no dating for me, he explained. Some of my romantic dreams were fed secretly on summer nights when the windows were open, and I could hear the Barbershop Quartet (who hung around the livery stable next to Finelli's grocery) harmonize. I lay in bed and listened to them, and was carried into "Wee Bonny Braes" in Scotland, down to Swanee River and other places. Even with this music, the summer was long and boring, so I was glad when school started in Louisville, and I was enrolled in Louisville Girls' High.

The size of the school amazed me. The first day I got lost in the halls and until the time I left, I still had to watch the turns to find the right room. Instead of having two grades in each room we had a different room for each subject and a special teacher, too.

Twice a week we went to the gymnasium for Physical Education. When Papa found out that folk dancing was to be one of the exercises he protested volubly, and refused to allow me to be a partaker in the devil's work.

One of the best things about going to school in Louisville was the ride of fifteen miles each day on the trolley. Going in was fun enough, but coming home every afternoon with the *Louisville Courier Journal*'s editor, Henry Watterson, across the aisle was really thrilling. Through his "Letters to the Editor," Papa had many encounters with Mr. Watterson, since they held opposite viewpoints on many issues. They disagreed on some facets of politics, the liquor question, and involvement in war. Papa challenged Mr. Watterson to open debate on some issues, which Mr. Watterson declined; but he invited Papa to write editorials in the *Courier Journal* on whatever subject he chose. Papa did, and several columns in the *Journal* were filled with Papa's ideas, many refuting editorials that had been written by Mr. Watterson. These Mr. Watterson also published.

I always rushed to get a seat across from Mr. Watterson on the trolley. He had a mustache, white as his hair. His eyes darted fire, it seemed to me, and when he read the newspaper, which he did on the car, he literally seemed to devour it paragraph by paragraph. He read one paragraph like I read one word; he seemed to read it in gulps.

The first six weeks in Louisville Girls' High School passed so quickly and happily that Conference time crept up on us before we knew it. The Louisville teachers were so different from those I'd known, who seldom if ever left the narrow confines of their own

160

counties. These instructors told about trips as far away as New York, and one enthralled us telling of her trip to Europe. They didn't dress like teachers, either. Instead of the regulation uniform of stiff starched shirtwaists and wool skirts, these ladies wore frilly dresses, and did their hair in exotic styles. They opened a new world to me.

Since Conference was held that year in Louisville, Mama and I could attend. We listened to all the speeches by outstanding preachers, but the last afternoon was the time we were anxiously awaiting. That was when appointments were read out. The names were read alphabetically. It wasn't long (Papa's name beginning with "C") before we heard "J. T. Cherry-Sebree." Mama and I gasped. Surely we couldn't be leaving Jeffersontown after just one year! Our city days were over. I began to sob, and looked at Mama to see if what I'd heard was true. It was. She was crying too, and Mama must have been upset, for that was the first time I had ever seen her weep in public. She must have been grieving for many things. Their savings was gone, and the move would be costly. In one of her rare demonstrative moments, Mama put her arm around me and whispered, "Willard (this time I let my name pass), I'm sorry, too. I wanted so many things for you."

Papa came to us then, and I could see that he, also, was disappointed. Angry, too. "This is my last appointment," he said earnestly. "Next year I'll superannuate. Enough is enough."

When we got home I looked up Sebree on the map. Just as I thought, it was about as far from Jeffersontown as it could get to still be in the Louisville Conference. Not a river in sight, not a lovely big city like Louisville to explore. Probably another two-room school with four grades in each room. What kind of a high school could such a place have? Then I had a comforting thought. Maybe in Sebree I might be able to share my own sophisticated ways, and impress the poor students who hadn't had my opportunities to live a worldly life. After all, I'd be doing something to enlighten the world.

So, in a magnanimous mood, I began to help Mama pack the linens and dishes and clothes and all the boxes of *The Tithe Law* for our move to Sebree.

29

Sebree

WE left Jeffersontown reluctantly, expecting little when we reached Sebree. How could any place compare with the wonderful new life we had enjoyed in Jeffersontown? We decided that we were leaving paradise for the desert.

To our surprise we found the parsonage in Sebree very attractive. It had been painted a mellow yellow and was nicely built, with two rooms and a hall in front, and three rooms behind. There were three bedrooms upstairs and a porch both downstairs and upstairs. Papa immediately went to the back to find out about a place for his garden and when he saw a large space set aside for this he was delighted.

We had a short time to get the furniture into the

house before there came a knock on the door our second night and a crowd of people came into the room calling out, "Surprise!"

There were no chairs set in place as yet, but the people did not seem to care. They laid their offerings, every shape and size, wherever they could find a space. I had never seen so much brought to us before at one time, and it was hard to wait until they left to poke into the bundles. Everything a person could imagine was there, from fresh food and meat to canned fruit and vegetables. There were also kitchen towels and washcloths, pots and pans, and other household necessities. We were very tired after putting all the perishables away. I went to bed upstairs and looked out the window. The moon was shining in its October style, making a path down the road in front and lighting the house across the street. Maybe, I thought sleepily, Sebree would be better than I'd expected.

Since all ministers had to move in October, school had been in session six weeks before we arrived, which meant facing a new gamut of curious eyes the first day. My courses of study did not always coincide with my previous one, so I had to catch up on back work many times. This was my freshman year in high school and I wondered about the teacher we would have, the students, and the building.

Papa went with me the first day. He always liked to meet the principal and teachers. We found that the building was set on a high hill overlooking the town. It was rather large, had two stories, and did not look too dilapidated. Steps led to the front entrance and we entered the hall. Evidently we had been expected, for the principal came out of his office at one side and extended his hand.

"You must be Brother Cherry, the new Methodist minister. This is your daughter?" He shook my hand rather limply. "What grade will she be in?"

I spoke up proudly. "I'm a freshman in high school. I came from Louisville—" I wanted this fact to impress him, but it didn't. He motioned to a girl passing by and said, "Show Brother Cherry and his daughter the way to Mrs. Kiser's room."

We walked up the flight of stairs in the middle of the hall and entered a large sunny room. It had double desks and the students were already seated. I looked around to see which seats were empty. There was one near the back, and after shaking hands, Mrs. Kiser led me to the desk. "This is Georgia. She will be your seatmate." We eyed each other a bit warily. A school year was a long time to share a seat with one person, but at least this was no one room schoolhouse as I had feared.

After school I walked to the post office in town. It gave me a chance to look over the stores. They were lined up on the two sides of the street and looked a lot like those in Calhoun. Nothing, of course, like the emporiums we saw in Louisville. I'd gone a step backward here.

Grandma Cherry came to visit us in Sebree that spring. She was very old then but her mind was alert and I found many things to talk over with her. She worried about my not having a regular sweetheart. I was getting on toward sixteen, and girls in her day were married by then. I just didn't seem to be interested. She often pressed me for an answer. "Aren't there any of these boys you like?"

One day in church Papa preached a moving sermon, conscious of Grandma sitting in the second pew, her eyes lighted with joy at hearing her chosen son preach. When he gave the invitation Grandma came up the aisle to the altar, clapping her hands and shouting. Tears were running down her cheeks. Grandma was in Papa's arms now and both of them were crying with joy. All around me other people were crying too, and I felt tears running down my face. I decided that Grandma's shouting made sense because of the way she lived. She really had something to shout *about*.

The summer we were in Sebree I was invited to visit one of the families who attended Papa's country church, the Dunvilles. It was there that I learned to make yeast bread, and it was there that I met the son Ralph, who had been away that winter at the Methodist prep school in Elkton. It was my first really serious love affair, for Ralph was a handsome boy, and most interesting. I was sorry to hear that he planned to return to Elkton to school that fall. How could I do without seeing him for such a long time?

Conference time came as usual in October. Papa had told us over and over that he planned to retire that session. We would move to Elkton and the thought filled me with joy, for I'd attend the same school Ralph was in and, now that I was allowed to date, we could see each other often.

Mama and I waited anxiously for Papa to come home from Conference, and when he did, we knew when we saw him that he had been granted his wish.

"I'm superannuated," he told us. "At last."

Once again we packed our things and left for Elkton to begin life for the first time as ordinary people, not a preacher's family. Maybe now, I hoped, so much would not be expected of me, and I could live like other girls.

30

We Pitch Our Tent

NOW Papa could at last experience release from the pressures brought about by dependence upon his parishioners for support. He looked forward to the independence he would have in making his own living. Papa had served thirty-two years in the itinerant ministry and he felt that at sixty-two he had a right to begin his new life as a free man.

We made the move from Sebree by train. We changed in Guthrie, boarded the dinky which ran between the two towns twice a day, and arrived at nine-thirty at night. A crowd of young people were at the station and I heard later that it was their custom to come by to see who was getting off. Papa, Mama, and I were the only passengers that time and I paid little attention to the crowd, for it had been a tiring trip. (Years later the man I married told me that he had gone home that night from the depot and said to his mother, "I saw the girl I'm going to marry get off the train tonight.") I was too excited over the prospect of seeing Ralph again to notice anyone.

Arms loaded with valises and bundles (Mama could never get everything into our suitcases), we made our way to the only hotel in town and rented a room. Papa fumed over the exorbitant price of a dollar a night and the next day he found a small house near his land and rented it. We had to stay in the hotel until our furniture arrived, so my start in school was delayed a few days.

We unpacked only the furniture we had to have, for Papa was very unhappy about spending ten dollars a month just for rent. He had told Uncle T.C. about the move he planned and Uncle T.C. had shipped a big tent to him via rail. One day it got there and Papa came by the house with a big bundle in a rented wagon. He stopped the mule and called to Mama and me, "Get in the wagon."

When we did we saw that some two-by-fours and rough planks were in the wagon too. Papa drove to his place, hitched the mule to a sapling, and began to unload. There were two huge maple trees standing at one side of the lot and Papa placed the two-by-fours near them. With our help he unrolled the tent and spread it on the ground.

Papa built a platform and set up the poles to hold the tent. Mr. Hunter, one of our neighbors, came to help and Papa hired him on the spot for a dollar a day to help build the house.

"Now we can move into our own place," Papa breathed a sigh of relief. "But you must get into school right away. You can start tomorrow."

I was enrolled as a sophomore and quickly discovered that John Locke offered no simple high school curriculum. My course called for Latin, which I'd had in Sebree the previous year, Greek, history, Bible, algebra, and physical geography. The subjects overwhelmed me. I wasn't too far behind in anything but Greek, but with the rest of the class almost seven weeks study ahead, I almost despaired. My teacher in both Greek and Latin was "Daddy" Whitten and he took some extra time to help me catch up. Four A.M. found me busy at work, sometimes reduced to tears. Mama's assurance, "One day it will come clear to you" was hard to believe, but one day Greek clicked and began to take an orderly place in my mind. Algebra posed a few problems too, but Ralph helped me here, being a whiz in this subject.

One afternoon when I got home, I found the house empty and went out to the place where our tent was pitched. The furniture had been set up inside. The back wall had a piece of tin inserted for the stovepipe, and Mama's Majestic range, a table, dining chairs, a piesafe, a stand for a waterbucket and pan, and a cupboard filled a large area. Two beds had been set up, the wardrobe for holding our best clothes, a table with a reading lamp, and rockers were in place. A lantern hung from a beam over the kitchen area.

Mama was cooking supper. I asked "How can we keep animals out? How can we heat the tent?" For once Mama didn't seem to have much to say except, "We'll wait and see."

Papa and Mr. Hunter were busy starting the foundation for the house. It was mid-October and winter would soon be upon us. I shivered at the thought of a Kentucky blizzard in a tent.

Our tent was a popular place on Sunday afternoons, the only time John Locke allowed for dating. Ralph came early and was a bit disgruntled when several of the boys from school followed him. Very soon other girls brought their dates too and we popped corn, made candy on the range, took pictures with our small cameras, and went for long walks together. There never seemed to be time enough to do all the things we planned.

Ralph was frustrated when a handsome senior started walking home with me every afternoon after school. No one was allowed this privilege but seniors, and Walton took full advantage of this. I had a hard time deciding between the boys. I knew I'd have to, for during that era girls only dated one boy at a time.

It was fortunate that we had a late fall. Papa and Mr. Hunter quickly put up the frame for the house and added weatherboarding. A man came out and built the double fireplace between the two front rooms and the flue for the kitchen chimney. Floors were laid upstairs and down, windows and doors added. We began to move inside when the windows were nailed in place. Papa had used the money he'd set aside for this part of the building and would have to wait until his pension came in the next fall to do more.

Fortunately, it didn't begin to snow until after Christmas. The weatherboarding offered little hindrance to the wind, which whistled through the cracks, and the first morning when I awakened to find snow on my bed, I shook it off the top quilt, and found that it was too cold in my room for the snow to melt.

My girl friends, used to heated rooms, often shivered with me between the cold sheets or huddled close to the fire. We talked endlessly about our futures, our boyfriends, our teachers, or people we knew. Occasionally we dated together for some social in town. When this happened I had a standing invitation to spend the night with them. They often loaned me a blouse to wear for some special occasion, too, for my wardrobe was scanty. I'd grown the past year and my clothes added little to my figure. Somehow I survived the winter, in fact, all of us enjoyed the challenge it brought.

That summer some of my sisters came home for a visit. It was a summer of work. Most of my friends spent their vacations in another town with relatives. School was out, the boys were gone, and, to pass the time, I dreamed of the past and the future. I lived again the senior banquet Walton had taken me to, for I was the only sophomore girl to be invited, either from John Locke or the local high school. It was taken for granted that I was Walton's girl. One of my affluent friends loaned me a lovely georgette crepe blouse, beaded all over, for the occasion. I spent the night at her house and she helped me dress and fixed my hair. The banquet was held in the hotel dining room, and it looked beautiful to me with its long tables covered with white cloths and set with silver and tall glasses with stiff pleated napkins like fans extending from the tops.

Walton was leaving that fall for college, he said. I'd miss him, of course, I assured him. But I thought secretly that any promise to remain his girl would not be fair. Who knew what boy might turn up at John Locke in my junior year?

31

Papa and the Rooster

PAPA could never stand waste in any form. One of his favorite parables was the story of the talents. He had preached on it from every pulpit in all of his churches. Whenever he encountered someone who failed to use some gift God had bestowed on him, he preached it again. Woe unto any one of us who used bad grammar, or who used a word incorrectly!

"Why do you think God gave you a good mind?" he would thunder at us. "Not to butcher the language."

Any work assigned to us through the years, if sloppily done or unfinished, brought forth his sermonette, too. He still challenged me constantly with new ways to grow mentally, physically, and spiritually. Only the best was expected of me and I often despaired of ever reaching the high goal Papa set for me.

I knew the day I saw him eyeing the hen sitting on a nest of eggs that something was on his mind. I didn't quite know what it was, but knowing his reasoning, I watched to see.

In the kitchen I heard him talking to Mama.

"How many hens do you have sitting?" he asked.

Mama stopped stirring the gravy on the stove and

stood moving her lips, counting. Then she said proudly, "Four now."

I could almost taste the first fried chicken that would come from the chicks she was hatching. All winter long about the only fresh meat we had was either at hog killing time, a wild rabbit someone brought, or an old hen past her useful time for laying eggs. On special occasions we bought steak from the butcher when we had an extra dime or two.

Papa scratched his head thoughtfully, and began to talk to himself.

"Broody hens don't lay. After the eggs are fertilized the roosters do nothing." His eyes brightened suddenly. "If the roosters could be made to sit on the eggs, it would save an enormous waste. As soon as a hen gets broody all you need to do is dunk her in cold water, put her in a cage for a day or two without food, and she won't waste much time before she starts laying eggs again. Think of the wasted production time!"

I wondered why ˙ ͜ ͜ ͜ sighed and why she was so quiet during the noon meal.

Papa went to his workshop where he used his own talent for carpentry. I followed him. He began to build a wooden cage which fitted over a hen's nest snugly, and I wondered what he was up to. It had never been hard to keep the hens on the nest, though sometimes they were disturbed by other hens trying to add an egg to their litter. Since Mama dated all the eggs with crayons, it was easy to remove the fresh ones, if the old hen cooperated. If she resented our intrusion with a vicious peck that often brought blood, it wasn't quite that easy. We found that a heavy glove slipped over our hand did the trick.

When Papa's cage was finished he took it to the henhouse. Carefully he fitted it over one of the sitting hens' nest. But when he removed it and went outside I began to wonder if my surmise was correct. He got an ear of corn from the crib and began to shell it, calling the chickens. At first they held back, unaccustomed to this extra feeding in the middle of the day, but as the corn fell, the bigger rooster called his harem, offering them this special bonus, taking the attitude that all good things came from him.

Papa swooped the rooster up into his arms and went into the henhouse.

"Take the hen off the nest and hold her."

Since she was one of the gentler ones, I did. Papa set the rooster on the nest and placed the cage over him. Immediately he stood up, his feathers barely touching the eggs.

"H-m-m-m, I'll have to make the cage lower."

When this was done, Papa again put the rooster on the eggs. The cage touched his back, and he started a mighty thrashing as he crouched in an uncomfortable position, squawking and touching the eggs as lightly as possible. His spurs cracked some of the eggs and when Papa saw that, he removed the cage, took the rooster out to the chopping block, and lopped off his head. He handed me the cage and went for hot water to scald the bird.

"Tell your mammy we'll have rooster tomorrow."

And that was when Mama invented her "Tough Old Rooster Casserole."

The Comforter

BY the end of the first summer Papa had almost reached his goal of supporting his family with food. We were faring well, with the expectation of faring even better when the hog Papa was raising was butchered in the fall. Papa had bought a goat to clean up the side of his place that was full of thorn trees and honeysuckle vines.

"A goat is the cheapest and best land-clearer that exists," he told us. "They eat everything and really clean out the brush."

One night as we were sitting together, Papa said, "Now if I can think of some way to furnish our clothes off the place, I'll be really independent."

Mama sighed and began to hum under her breath her song, "His grace is enough for me. . . ." I'd learned long ago to expect something unusual when she did this and next day I saw Papa standing outside very still. He was eyeing the goat. When he saw me he said, "One of these days I'd like to make all our clothes out of goat skins. Then we could live entirely off the land."

Next day he sheared the goat. He brought the wool to the back door and called to Mama. When she saw it she looked a bit apprehensive.

"I'm going to make a comforter out of it," he said.
Mama sniffed the wool. "It smells terrible."

"I'll wash it," Papa promised.

After the wool was washed, dried, and carded, it was placed between two sheets of unbleached muslin and tacked in place. It soon got cool and Papa proudly spread the comforter over the bed.

It rained that night and the smell of goat pervaded the house. I heard both of my parents walking restlessly around downstairs. In the morning I noticed that the comforter was in the kitchen. Mama was talking, "Those hairs pricked me to pieces," she complained.

"I'll take care of that," Papa promised. He left for town and when he returned he handed Mama a big bundle. "Put the comforter between this ticking. The hairs can't creep out then."

Reluctantly Mama tacked it inside, a doubtful look on her face. That night it rained again, and the smell of goat became quite pungent. I heard Mama coming up the stairs. She got into my bed. This was an unprecedented event and I asked her, "What happened?"

Mama chuckled. "Those hairs are alive. They came through that ticking like it wasn't there. My skin feels like a pin cushion."

Next morning the comforter was gone. We didn't ask Papa what he had done with it. The only clue I had was a freshly dug mound of dirt in the back lot. That afternoon Papa gave me some money and told me to go to town and buy material for a new school dress. "In a way," he seemed to be comforting himself, "the money to buy it came from the place."

The dress would look nicer, I thought, smiling to

myself, than Papa's dream of our being dressed like Elijah, "girt with a girdle of leather about his loins" (2 Kgs. 1:8).

Junior Year

SEPTEMBER came, and it was again time to enter school. The first day always held its share of anticipation at John Locke. It was exciting to discover what new boys might be entering. Sometimes they came from another state.

I walked into the chapel, looking over the crowd. I wore my hair in a long braid down the middle of my back. It was tied at the neck with a big bow of ribbon. Scanning the students, m........ fastened on a slender young man. His eyes and hair were very dark, his complexion very fair. I wondered at the combination. The boy seated behind me saw me looking at him and whispered, "He's from Brazil. His name is Reginald Dealtry."

Brazil. That faraway land! I remembered one summer in Calhoun when missionaries from Brazil had been home on furlough for a visit. The Joiner children played with us many afternoons. When they got excited they lapsed into Portuguese, a habit I encouraged. I'd learned a few words, and I wondered if Reginald spoke Portuguese too.

When chapel was over, I started to my first class,

pretending I didn't see Reginald walking beside me.

"Franceesca." His voice was beautiful, and the way he said "Frances" pleased me. "It is—" he touched my braid. My heart pounding with joy. "Franceesca, it is—" his broken English failed to supply the word he needed so Harry, who was walking by, furnished it for him.

"Red," he teased, "bright red." He gave my braid a yank and went on. Inwardly I fumed. Most of the boys treated me like they owned me, trying to boss me around. What would Reginald think?

There was little teasing after that, for Reginald took over every available minute of my time he could. He walked me to classes, seeing that I sat at the end of the long recitation bench, and taking his place beside me. We dated every Sunday afternoon. The first time he came I was a little worried about what he would think about my home, for we had learned that Reginald's father was a millionaire, and I knew his surroundings had to be different from mine. The room in which I entertained him was still unfinished inside, with only the weatherboarding standing between us and the elements. Papa had some qualms when he learned that Reginald was a Catholic, too, but when he attended our Methodist church every Sunday he began to feel less anxious. Papa gave me dire warnings about the perfidy of that denomination, but he must have known that nothing he said would change my mind. For the very first time, real love had entered my life. I knew that past attractions had been nothing in comparison.

Mama confined her feeling to an occasional comment, but the day Reginald put his arm around her shoulder, kissed her cheek, and said, "Our Franceesca is a wonderful girl," she was won over. She continued to turn Reginald's picture on my dresser upside down every time she passed by it, but that was her way of telling me that she understood and cared.

We were both seventeen that year, and greedy for all of our time together. Every afternoon Reginald ran past our house for exercise and I always knew there would be a note from him in the mailbox. Of course there was one from me to him too. Nights we signaled to each other from our rooms upstairs, for we had discovered that the distance between my home and the school was only a mile across the open field.

As the year drew near the end we were so desperate at the thought of parting that we were almost ill. Reginald wrote to his uncle in Louisville who was his guardian while he was in the States for money to buy an engagement ring for me. I didn't know this until later on in the summer when "Mike's" (a co-principal of John Locke School) wife told me that he had, and that the Uncle, alarmed that I might be trying to "take" Reginald for some money, called the school. He was assured that I had no such idea in mind but he sent very little money to Reginald from then on, which made impossible any idea we may have entertained about eloping.

The day Reginald came to say goodbye, he kissed Mama again, shook Papa's hand, and put his arm around my shoulder. Papa cleared his throat as he looked at us, and both his and Mama's eyes were filled with tears. My own were spilling over, and Reginald, too, was crying. Papa and Mama left us alone then and we frankly wept in each other's arms. I thought my heart would break as I watched him walking away down the road to town.

Reginald came back late that summer to get his transcripts to another school. He was planning to be an engineer, and this year had been set aside especially to learn English in our small place. We spent the day together, and as night came on Mama handed us a small bunch of mint. It was dried up and withered, but she said, "Plant it by the pond and if it grows it will prove that your love is real."

"It will grow," Reginald said confidently.

The mint grew through the years, green and fragrant, but even as we planted it I knew that every time I smelled mint it would bring a memory of a precious time to be cherished in memory but never again to be relived.

Life isn't always fair to seventeen-year-olds.

34

Second Summer

THE second summer we were on Papa's place was, fortunately, a busy one for all of us. Mama planted more flower beds in the yard, set out the rose slips she had started the fall before, and added a row of dahlias to Papa's garden. Mama had a way with growing things and she never hesitated to ask for some bulb, seed, or slip that pleased her. Her pansy bed was a riot of color in the spring and the fragrance of Sweet Betsy pervaded the whole yard.

Mama's sister, my Aunt Connie Elrod, lived in

Bowling Green. She had a large acreage planted in strawberries, and invited me to come and help during the picking season.

Aunt Connie had three boys in her family and fed many of the workers. She asked me if I would take over the noon meal instead of working in the berry patch. There were at least twenty to feed and I proudly showed my prowess at the cookstove. All the things I had learned in domestic science came in here, and the hours Mama had taught me through the years returned to my aid. Afternoons I packed berries in the shed and learned the art so well that I had no trouble getting a job the next spring. The earnings furnished my school clothes. Aunt Connie and Uncle Elrod were generous. In fact, they wanted me to come and live with them. The three boys begged me to come too. They promised me a college education, music, and other benefits if I would. I had never thought Mama really thought too much of me but when she heard, she threw her ___ ind me and said, in the rarest moment in ou relationship, "I never want to have you go away again!"

Chautauqua was scheduled that summer in Elkton and it started a little while after my return. Papa bought a family ticket which permitted us to go to every session. A big tent had been set up at the edge of town with rows of benches and a raised platform. The floor was covered with sawdust and when you entered the door the scent of damply trampled grass assailed your nostrils. It carried a kind of heady circus smell and I was thrilled to be part of the audience. There was one fly in my ointment, though. I was very conscious of the impression I made and on my way to the Chautauqua every day I was joined by Rebecca, whose mental ability only reached the second grade. She was tall and awkward, and her grin gave away her I.Q. Worst of all, her hair was red like mine and I was afraid that the people who ran the Chautauqua would think she was my sister. Since Rebecca depended on me for washing her hair and helping her with problems she could not handle alone, I couldn't hurt her feelings, but inwardly I was humiliated. I did want to make a good impression.

Chautauqua offered a variety of entertainment. Lectures, which we younger ones only endured, were frequent. We had comedy, Shakespearean drama, and magicians like Blackstone, who amazed us with his ability. The best performance of all was an orchestra which ended the program with the Anvil Chorus. Lights were dimmed, and a spotlight was turned on the back of the stage where a blacksmith stood at his anvil with a huge sledgehammer. In time to the music he struck the iron and sparks flew up like shooting stars. We felt that the week had been well spent.

35

Graduation

WHEN time came for school to start I was sad, for I knew that Reginald would not be there. It seemed impossible that anyone could take his place and looking over the boys at school confirmed my impression.

One of the students was from the Kentucky mountains. He was tall, gangly, and his coat sleeves hung halfway between his elbows and wrists. He entered the chapel the first day carrying a plug of tobacco in his mouth, as was the custom in the hills where he lived. The teachers soon persuaded him to give up this habit which, they explained, was not a good one for a ministerial candidate. He had graduated from the eighth grade, he told us, and was far behind in his studies. Every needy person touched my heart and always had, and I offered to coach Floyd. My teachers were pleased and let us have special time to work. My senior year was made much better because of this, for I saw Floyd improve in so many ways. He began to dress better, his English became good, and he seemed more at ease at social gatherings. He was a remarkable student, catching up with his class before the year passed. He became a bishop in the Methodist Conference in later years.

Before I knew, it was time for school to close. night of graduation arrived. It was to be held in church. Reluctantly I donned the dress set aside for occasion, looking critically at it in the mirror. Elizabeth, who had become a nurse and was living in Louisville, had gotten it in a box of clothes donated by one of her friends and had sent it to me. It was made of net ruffles, which covered it from top to hem. It did little for my plump figure, but it was white, the color girls always wore for this occasion. I comforted myself with the thought of the bouquet of flowers our wealthy friend had promised to send. I had helped her many times in her home and I thought that she would send something beautiful as a kind of thanks.

Two other girls were graduating too, and as I

compared my dress to theirs I decided that I was plain tacky. We marched into the choir loft and I was thankful for the high partition around the seats. I sat as low as I could, trying to attract as little notice as possible.

The door opened at the back of the church and three boys came down the aisle carrying our flowers. From a distance all the sprays looked pretty but as they approached the front the scent of dog fennel assailed my nostrils. I knew then that no hothouse flowers were to be mine. My wealthy friend, with her usual frugality, had had her Indian servant go into the fields and pick the lacy weed and wild daisies. She had not even used real ribbon. A strip of white crepe paper had been tied around the stems. Harry, who always teased me unmercifully, held his nose and snickered. I wanted to die. When the ceremony was over I put the flowers in my seat and left the church as quickly as I could. Mama, Papa, and I walked the long way home, saying little. Neither one asked me about the bouquet. Even Papa, who ridiculed all forms of pride, seemed to sympathize with me.

Now that I was a graduate, I wondered what life would bring, especially after that inauspicious beginning.

36

Fulfillment

PAPA seemed to blossom as he worked under his "own vine and fig tree" (1 Kgs 4:25). The restlessness brought about when Sunday came and he didn't stand in the pulpit was somewhat assuaged by teaching the adult Bible class in the Methodist Church, performing wedding ceremonies at his house, and counseling many who came to him for advice. The extra money which came from fees for marriages helped our finances. One afternoon a bashful young man and his fiancee came to the door to be married. Papa, as usual, questioned them about the way they felt toward each other, and asked if either had been divorced (he refused to marry anyone who had). When the ceremony was over, the man, who stuttered, asked Papa, "Brother Cherry, is it k-k-kistomary to k-k-kuss the bride?"

One afternoon Papa was called to see one of our friends who was dying. When he returned his face had a troubled look. I knew the family and had loved the man. His wife was the greediest person I ever knew and one of the most cruel. When we lived in Elkton the first time, I had seen her force the black girl who lived with her to remove coffee grounds from the pig slop bucket and eat them because she had not boiled all the strength out of them. She also had an Indian woman servant who lived with her and loved snuff and tobacco. About the only thing I could see that the Indian woman got out of the money that came to her from her Oklahoma reservation was enough to chew. Her clothes were always secondhand and ragged, and she ate whatever scraps were left from the table. So I wondered if the man might not have wanted to tell Papa about his part in these things before he died. Finally I asked Papa, "What happened?"

I could tell that he was deeply distressed. "Every time he started to say something to me, his wife interrupted him and told him he must be quiet. He never was allowed to open his heart to me before she made me leave the room. What a way to die!"

Papa worked hard outside until noon, when he came inside and studied during the heat of the day. He had filled two sides of the dining room with his books, and with a pile of them beside him he sat in his big old-fashioned rocker before the window with a lapboard across the chair arms, reading, writing articles which were published in newspapers and church papers. He spent hours preparing his Sunday school lessons, writing letters to his brothers, children, and friends. Many times Uncle H.H., who was now president of the college he established in Bowling Green, came by for a long talk and advice, especially when some political problem stared him in the face. One minister who discovered that his wife had been unfaithful came to Papa one day for advice. It must have been good, for the man and his wife left the town for a western city and we heard later that they were getting along well.

Papa and Mama shared their hospitality with their friends. We never knew who might stop by at any time of the day to share a meal or spend the night. As they sat on the porch Mama would bring out goblets of her fresh churned buttermilk, cold from the icebox. In season Papa cut melons in the yard outside and once a year everyone who wanted to come was invited for a watermelon feast under the maple trees. Mama kept a big gourd of coarse salt to sprinkle on the fruit, as she raised gourds as her special project.

Papa never stopped being a preacher. When my sisters came for visits he always held a parting ceremony before they left. One of his favorite passages he used at that time was 1 Corinthians 13, the love chapter. I usually sat on the stairs where I could hide my tears in the dimness, for seeing my relatives leave brought a lot of sadness, especially after my nieces and nephews made their appearances. I was so proud of being an aunt, though there were not too many years difference in age between the oldest one and myself. None of my sisters ever cried in public; keeping emotions in control was considered a part of being ladylike. I decided that I wasn't a lady anyhow, so I blubbered away to their disgust. Papa's life was a happy one, living in the best of two worlds as a minister and a free man.

World War I

ALL during my senior year there had been rumblings of war in Europe but it was almost summer before we began to feel the foreboding of a dark cloud of disaster hovering over us. How long, our elders began to ask, could we stand by and see smaller nations overrun by Germany? Editorials were written urging our participation. Ministers preached from the pulpit; politicians made flowery speeches full of promises about the way they, if elected, would handle the situation.

The sinking of the British liner, the *Lusitania*, with many Americans aboard infuriated us. It led to the declaration of war by Congress on April 4, 1917, two years later. At first it was hoped that the help from the United States could be confined to sending materials and food supplies. The war was across the ocean and we didn't think that our men might be needed too until Congress passed the Selective Service Act in 1917. It called for men twenty-one to thirty years of age. As more men were needed the age was changed to eighteen to forty-five, and the war came home to us, for it was taking a toll from every kind of occupation, teachers, students, and others. Stamps jumped from two cents to three cents, a rise in costs we patriotically accepted. Liberty loans were urged in special meetings. Girls were urged to join the nursing force and, filled with patriotism, I volunteered my service after I graduated.

I was turned down upon examination by our family doctor who announced that I had a heart murmur which would keep me out. I often wondered if Papa and Mama, who were on very friendly terms with Dr. Weathers, had anything to do with that decision. I knew, of course, that my heart had been broken when Reginald left, but outside of that it seemed to me to be functioning well. So I had to occupy my time helping the Red Cross roll bandages and encouraging my friends whose brothers and sweethearts had been drafted to "smile," though the popular song admitted that "your heart is breaking." I pointed out to them that "Over There" was a glamorous place to be. "Keep the Home Fires Burning," we sang as we went with some of the girls and their families to the depot to see their men off to camp. We tried to comfort them with the assurance that this was a righteous war and that it would end all wars. "Think what your loved ones are doing for our country!" was our battle cry.

Nell, on her last visit home, had left me her Victrola. No longer did I play one of the three records she gave me. They were laid aside for "On Flanders Fields," "K-K-Katie," and others.

Nell had volunteered for work as a Red Cross secretary. She was in Russia. Elizabeth was a Red Cross nurse in France. Their letters told of their adventures overseas and I often felt left out with a life ahead of me and nothing to do. Even the glamor of a nursing career had been denied me.

John Locke had lost several of its teachers, and when it came time to open in the fall, the board asked me if I would teach there. I thought of the boys with whom I'd gone to school the past years and felt a lot of reluctance about taking this position. One of the boys returning was Harry, who had plagued me through my stay at the school every time he could. It was good to know that there would be some new younger students. Maybe I could manage them at least.

Papa was to teach Bible, and Mama was asked to manage the dining room and one dormitory. Mama and I moved into two of the upstairs rooms and Papa stayed at his place, coming in every day for classes and to eat his noon meal. It was a real sacrifice for him, but it was a time when everyone was expected to fall in and help in every way he could.

I was to teach Latin and Physical Geography. The day I entered the room where my first class was to be held one of the boys spoke up, "How about a date tonight?" The others laughed. I blushed a fiery red.

"Now her face is the same color as her hair," Harry remarked.

What should I do? I had been warned by the chairman of the school board who was also our local pastor not to be on familiar terms with the boys. I gave Harry what I hoped was a severe look, opened my book, and started the lesson with what I labeled as dignified assurance. My salary was to be thirty-five dollars a month, a sum which looked very large to me.

The school was undergoing some repairs. New paper was being hung, ceilings painted, and floors redone. I noticed a very tall man who was overseeing the work. He was one of the town boys, Seaton Cartwright. Every time I passed by he tried to say something to me, but I ignored him completely. I knew he was the same one who had tried to trick me into coming to his cousin's home the summer before so that he could drop by and meet me. All I knew about him was that he didn't go with the town set to which I belonged. He lived with his widowed mother he had quit school when he finished the sixth grade While none of these facts impressed me at all, I knew how my family would feel about this. There was rumor that he was fast, that he drank, and he smoked chain-fashion.

When his attempts to get my attention became obvious to Papa and Mama, they made some discreet inquiries about him which they passed on to me. They hoped to prevent the start of any kind of romance between us. They need not have worried about my interest, for I rather considered myself to be Walton's girl.

He had not waited to be drafted. Hearing the rumor of war, he volunteered early. One day he had come by our house to tell us he was going overseas. He led me into the room where Papa and Mama sat. "I don't feel that I have any right to ask Frances to wait for me. I might be crippled. But if I get home safe that will be another situation." He put his arm across my shoulders. "I do hope, Frances, if you find anyone you like better than you do me, you will let me see him before you make a final decision." He said to Papa and Mama, "Promise to keep Frances for me." Papa and Mama nodded. I made no promise, however. I just said "goodbye."

I felt very virtuous and patriotic being Walton's girl. To me he had expressed his love for his country in a tangible way. We exchanged letters. I tried to write him every week. His replies were erratic. The interference of U-boats stopped much of the ocean travel.

worried about Walton's safety. I knew he was holding a clerical job in France and that he was not lying in some horrible trench, but when I talked about him I just mentioned proudly that he was in France with the AEF (American Expeditionary Force). I comforted myself with trying to believe that, while my part in the war was not adventurous like the roles my sisters were playing, that at least my boyfriend over there was being supported by me. His morale was kept up by my loyalty to him, he wrote.

Soon boys began to return to the United States as casualties of war. They came home minus legs, arms, eyes, and crippled by shell shock. We began to question the glamor of this war. I talked to Papa about this. He remembered the Civil War, his sons had been in the Spanish American one, and now he was seeing the biggest war of all.

"Will this end all wars?" I asked Papa.

"As long as there is human greed and treachery men will fail to get along," he said. "Until we learn to love our neighbor as ourselves the way Jesus taught us, men will continue to quarrel. Human nature doesn't change much, and hasn't since earliest history." Papa sighed, remembering the wars he had lived through before, and seeing his descendants confronted forever with the same horror.

That winter the flu epidemic hit everywhere. Dr. Boone ordered John Locke quarantined until the epidemic was over, but the virus had already entered and many of the boys became ill. Mama, Papa, and I spent hours nursing our boys. I seemed to be immune from the disease and when two of the other teachers came down with it, I added more classes to my load. Headlines screamed "Twenty million cases of influenza in the States," and bold black type proclaimed, "Four hundred and thirty thousand deaths." Elkton had its share of casualties too. One day five from one family were buried. The undertakers kept on the go day and night. Fortunately, none of our students died.

Seaton had been hanging around me every time he had a chance. I thought that when Dr. Boone quarantined us I would get rid of him for awhile, but he asked, since he was working on the place, that he be quarantined too. I had begun to notice him oftener than I felt I should because of my commitment to Walton. My conscience pricked. Seaton, in spite of the fact that he had been declared 4-F status for the army, had something which attracted girls, I knew. He was six-feet-two, very slender. His eyes were dark and piercing. He was graceful and I was told that he had no peer when it came to dancing. His voice was soft and his smile could touch your heart. I tried not to let it.

My best friend advised me to leave him alone. "His reputation isn't good," she warned. "He has a way of leading a girl on until . . ." she stopped, embarrassed, letting me finish the sentence for myself, ". . . then dropping her."

I might have listened to all my advisors and to my conscientious duty to Walton if it had not been for the arrival of Halloween. This was a much celebrated day in Elkton. The young folks took the opportunity to do outlandish things that night. Once they put a cow in the courthouse steeple, and the owner had a hard time getting her down. Outside privies were discovered in a front yard blocks away from where they had been.

All of us walked the streets, even those who did not participate in the activities. Since my "steady" was overseas, one of my friends asked me to go with him. He had never asked me before, but thinking that under the circumstances I could go without betraying Walton, I consented. We started out and he led me to a dark alley on the other side of the town.

"Stay here a minute, I'll be right back," he said.

I stood for what seemed to me to be a long time alone in black darkness, wondering what had happened to Goebel. I could not see my hand before my face. I was beginning to get scared and very angry when I heard a voice nearby.

"Hi!" I recognized it as Seaton's. "What in the world are you doing here?"

I had to admit to myself that I was glad to see him, but I said sarcastically, "My friend Goebel gave me the slip." Being given the slip was an insult that was almost unforgivable.

I thought I heard a snicker from nearby. Seaton took my arm firmly and said sympathetically, "Let's get out of here. What a dirty trick!" His concern touched me. I found later that my first date with Seaton had cost him five dollars. That was the price Goebel had charged.

We walked back to the campus. We found that a prankster had moved someone's buggy near the gate on the campus. We sat in it and for the first time we talked. I found that he was 4-F because of his health. He had many interesting tales to tell. He had been up north to work and stories about such far-off cities as Akron intrigued me. I had hardly ever been outside of Kentucky.

Seaton took it for granted after that night that I was to be his girl. When the boys at John Locke realized this they took him aside to point out to him that whatever his way of life with girls had been in the past, his association with me had to be honorable. I heard that Harry, the leader of my tormentors, headed this group. When Seaton and I kept on dating, my friends in town tried, I think, to include us in their plans, but there was such a caste system in Elkton that it embarrassed them. Inwardly I sputtered at their attitude, and Seaton scoffed at their bigotry. It was he who finally refused to go to their parties and their homes.

Mama and Papa tried to tell me that there were better chances for my marriage than this one, for from the beginning Seaton's intentions were serious. He told everyone he planned to marry me. He never gave me a chance to change my mind.

My parents insisted that I write to Walton and tell him my plans, which I did. I didn't receive his reply until I returned from my honeymoon.

Seaton and I were married in September. My sisters did come to the wedding. They helped me buy my wedding suit, a gray serge. My shoes were a gray high buttoned style, my blouse was georgette crepe, beaded lavishly. My hat was velvet, also beaded. We stood before the fireplace in our living room, Papa and Mama at one side. Papa had refused to perform the ceremony. Our local minister did it instead. There were no smiling faces in that room. Seaton's mother was frankly crying. Mama's nose was twitching as it always did when she was disturbed. Papa's face looked like it was made of granite as he firmly held his emotions in check. Only Seaton stood proud and sure, and I felt his assurance that all would be well in our marriage.

The local taxi was waiting outside the gate to take us

to the station where we were leaving to go on our honeymoon in Chattanooga. We got in and for a moment I sat looking out the window.

The place had changed a lot in the four years since we had moved there. Fences were set wherever needed over the whole acreage. There was a big porch now across the whole front of the house, which was painted white. In the yard Mama's flower beds were growing where the tent had stood. The shade trees Papa had planted were casting shadows and the fruit trees were beginning to bear. The pasture in front of the yard was green and even. The two Jersey cows clipping grass completed the picture.

Papa's dream was coming true very fast, I thought. I was happy for him and for Mama.

The car started and I looked out of the window to wave goodbye. Papa sat in his big porch rocker, dressed in his best suit and looking like the Kentucky colonel I teased him about favoring. Mama sat nearby. She, too, was dressed in her best. They felt no want now for material things.

But I saw such a loneliness there that I had to turn away to hide my tears. Our happy days together as a family were gone forever, and another path was ahead for all of us to follow.

Epilogue
Carried to the Skies

PAPA lived on his place twenty years before he died. At the last it was hard for me to see Papa reduced to helplessness on a bed of pain. Through the years we had been so close. Through our ups and downs and disagreements and misunderstandings had come a realization of what we meant to each other.

Papa had mellowed now. His attitude was more loving to those with whom he couldn't, "in conscience," as he said, "agree." We sat for hours discussing some fine point. We read poetry. I listened to articles he wrote. Once again I let him call me "Willard," a name I'd abandoned in Jeffersontown for "Frances."

Elizabeth and I took turns nursing him for the last six months he lived. One day Papa called me to his bedside and confided that I didn't hurt him like the others did when I bathed him.

"Of all my children," he told me one day, "You are the only one who has never caused me a moment's pain."

I felt like crawling under the bed in shame. I, who had been guilty of laughing out loud at the bedside of a dying parishioner when a dog bumped the floor under me. I, who had been called forward to sit on the altar rail facing the audience because of misbehavior while Papa was preaching. I, who had stolen cheese and lied about it. I, who had defied Papa and Mama and made an unfortunate marriage, and brought home two girls to burden them. So many things I'd done, and Papa had forgotten them all. He must be remembering, I thought, the happy times when we had gone to his country appointments, sometimes walking through mud, sometimes riding in a buggy over the frozen roads. Or the hours we spent fishing and swimming. Papa's last thoughts held nothing but pleasant remembrances of me, and I was glad.

A week before Papa died he lapsed into a coma, and his last words to Mama and my sister were, "Take care of my Willard."

Papa looked so peaceful as he lay in his casket. He was wearing his best gray suit and I almost waited to hear him say, "I take for my text—" I threw myself across the foot of a bed and sobbed out all my hurt at his suffering the past six months.

"It just isn't fair, God," I cried out. "He didn't deserve it."

I was exhausted, and fell into a deep sleep. I could see Papa dressed in his best suit, walking straight and tall. His face was shining and his tenor voice was lifted as he sang in joy:

Must I be carried to the skies
On flowery beds of ease

When others fought to win the prize
And sailed through bloody seas?

And I knew that Papa's bloody seas had changed to smooth waters for his final sailing.

Some time had elapsed since the funeral. I walked behind the barn and the scent of pennyroyal came to me, bringing with it the memory of the times when Papa and I walked together; and especially our walk from the boat landing at Mouth of Gasper to Grandma's.

As we approached the barn I could see Papa stop, sniff, and answer my unspoken question before it was asked. "Pennyrile, so powerful you can almost hear it."

And I knew that, like the familiar scent of pennyroyal in Kentucky, Papa, too, would be heard in a lasting remembrance.

7